I love my books!
  They are companions dear,
    Sterling in worth,
     In friendship most sincere;
    Here talk I with
      The wise in ages gone,
       And with the nobly gifted
      Of our own.

— FRANCIS BENNOCH
From *My Books*

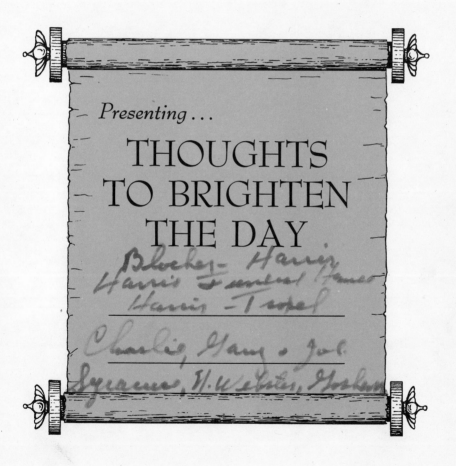

Presenting . . .

THOUGHTS
TO BRIGHTEN
THE DAY

Books in this inspirational series
distributed by Doubleday & Company, Inc.

The Joy of Words
The New Joy of Words
Words of Inspiration
Words of Wisdom
Words for All Seasons
The Gift of Words
Treasured Thoughts
Thoughts to Brighten the Day
A Treasury of Great American Quotations

THOUGHTS
TO BRIGHTEN
THE DAY

Selections from many sources
providing
reading for casual enjoyment
thoughts for patient perusal
and
unusual poetry and prose
to stimulate the imagination

Edited by
THOMAS C. JONES

Illustrated by
KAY LOVELACE SMITH

J. G. FERGUSON PUBLISHING COMPANY

CHICAGO

Distributed to the book trade by Doubleday & Company, Inc.

COMMENT BY THE EDITOR,
AND ACKNOWLEDGMENTS

For at least the next generation, the summer of 1969 will be remembered by mankind as the time of the moon landing. Poets, philosophers, astronomers, astrologists, scientists, musical composers, and writers of mystery stories have for centuries been inspired by the moon. Suddenly, man has been there and returned with lunar rock specimens. The world has lost one of its most persistent subjects of speculation but has gained a whole new universe for exploration.

Literature began with man's efforts to chronicle for others his new experiences and discoveries. From the earliest cultures, the songs, drawings, and writings of man have told of the romance and hardships of voyages—from the travels of Marco Polo to the amazing expedition of Lewis and Clark in their epic journey to the Pacific Ocean and the early voyages to the North Pole by Admiral Peary.

We have now entered the era of space exploration, which will ultimately penetrate beyond all known heavenly bodies. The literature of the future will reflect the great change in life on earth and concepts about future civilizations.

In *Thoughts to Brighten the Day* we have selected a variety of old favorite essays, poems, stories, and accounts of early exploration, to furnish the reader with samplings of the heritage of the past. Many of the ideas expressed by early authors are as true to life today as they were when written centuries ago. Possibly, to the more militant young readers this material is totally irrelevant. Nevertheless, we like to think that the traditions of the past will penetrate beyond the earth to whatever lies ahead.

By no means is the material in this volume restricted to familiar old favorites. We have purposely culled the libraries for unusual descriptions of early exploration and unique experiences. We believe that you will be entertained and amused by many of these interesting discoveries.

Furthermore, the first four pages, which are dedicated to the historic voyage to the moon, serve as a permanent souvenir of the landing, which must be acknowledged as *the event of the century*. This is certainly one of the first printings, in book form, of the most memorable quotations of the week of July 16 to 24, 1969.

We have been fortunate in receiving the cooperation of many authors and publishers in order to assemble such a variety of styles and periods of writing. From the most recent poem of Archibald MacLeish—*Voyage to the Moon*—to the essays of Plato and Marcus Aurelius, there are hundreds of thoughts to amuse and stimulate the reader.

For the advocate of the Victorian nineteenth century there are selections from Ella Wheeler Wilcox, John Greenleaf Whittier, Henry Wadsworth Longfellow, Abraham Lincoln, Mark Twain, Theodore Roosevelt, Bret Harte, and Frederic Remington. From the twentieth century there are such notables as Edgar A. Guest, John Steinbeck, Ernest Hemingway, John Gunther, Langston Hughes, Ogden Nash, Bruce Barton, Robert Frost, Elbert Hubbard, Herbert Hoover, Grantland Rice, and Will Rogers. There are eighteenth-century thinkers, such as Benjamin Franklin, Thomas Paine, and Thomas Jefferson.

The organization of the material into categories—*Thoughts from the Past and Present—Particularly for the Male—Words and Thoughts of Historical Interest—Especially for the Ladies—Comedy and Happy Thoughts*—only suggests the general nature of the subjects. We hope that readers of both genders will find items to interest them in every section.

In addition to thanking the publishers, authors, and other individuals who have given us permission to reprint this material, we wish to acknowledge the gracious assistance of specific individuals whose talents and industry have made this work possible. The sales and creative departments of Brown and Bigelow initiated the project and saw it through to completion. Harriet Helmer, my assistant, was an interested and patient editor of copy and persistent seeker of permissions. Kay Lovelace Smith, as illustrator, made the material more appealing with her original and puckish subject treatment. The A-1 Composition Company, our typesetter, cooperated with us in their usual efficient manner. Photopress, Inc., our lithographer, owned and operated by the Chalifoux family, took an ever patient and understanding approach to the problems of publishing. Al Josephson, with Photopress, lent a talented and inspired touch to final layout. Finally, the service rendered by Jim Stewart and A. C. Engdahl and Company, Inc., bookbinders, helped to get the book to the market for distribution to you, the reader.

We wish to acknowledge the permissions of publishers, authors, and other individuals as follows:

Atlantic-Little, Brown and Company—*Personal Prejudices*, from *England Reclaimed* by Sir Osbert Sitwell. Copyright 1948, 1949 by Sir Osbert Sitwell. By permission of Atlantic-Little, Brown and Company. The Bangor Daily News, Bangor, Maine—*Why a Boat Is a "She"*. A. S. Barnes & Company, Inc.—*The Answer* from *Only the Brave and Other Poems* by Grantland Rice. Copyright, 1941, by A. S. Barnes & Company, Inc. Randall Barton—*My Five Best Dinner Companions* by Bruce Barton. Albert and Charles Boni, Inc.—*Just Money Never Made Friends with Anybody* by Will Rogers from *Letters of a Self-Made Diplomat to His President*. Copyright, 1926, by Albert and Charles Boni, Inc. The Bobbs-Merrill Company, Inc.—*It's the Custom* from *All Things Considered* by Howard Vincent O'Brien, copyright 1948 by The Bobbs-Merrill Company, Inc., reprinted by permission of the

* * * * *

TABLE OF CONTENTS

Thoughts from the Past and Present

Particularly for the Male

TABLE OF CONTENTS

Words and Thoughts of Historical Interest

Especially for the Ladies

Comedy and Happy Thoughts

Thoughts from
the Past and Present
FROM THE POT-BELLIED STOVE
TO THE LUNAR LANDING

Historic Quotations from the Week the World Will Always Remember

Man's First Flight to the Moon

The spirit of the American people as well as the world will soar with you on your flight to the moon.

—President Richard M. Nixon

The Eagle has landed.

That's one small step for a man, one giant leap for mankind.

—Neil A. Armstrong, Mission Commander

I'd like to take this opportunity to ask every person listening in, whoever and wherever they may be, to pause for a moment and contemplate the events of the past few hours and to give thanks in his or her own way. *—Col. Edwin E. Aldrin Jr.*

* * * * *

During a televised appearance while returning from the epic voyage to the moon, each of the astronauts expressed his feelings concerning the historic event:

This trip of ours to the moon may have looked simple and easy. I want to assure you that this has not been the case.

The complex equipment that made the mission possible, from the Saturn 5 rocket for the launching to the guidance computer with its 38,000-word vocabulary, and the "blood, sweat and tears" of thousands of American workers, scientists and engineers all contributed to the success of this mission.

All you see is us, but below the surface are thousands and thousands of others, and to all of them I would like to say, "Thank you very much." *—Col. Michael Collins*

We've come to the conclusion that this has been far more than three men on a voyage to the moon, more still than the efforts of a government and industry team, more even than the efforts of one nation.

We feel that this stands as a symbol of the insatiable curiosity of all mankind to explore the unknown.

Neil's statement the other day upon first setting foot on the surface of the moon—*That's one small step for a man, one giant leap for mankind*—I believe sums up these feelings very nicely.

We accepted the challenge of flying to the moon. The acceptance of this challenge was inevitable. The relative ease with which we carried out our mission, I believe, is a tribute to the timeliness of that acceptance.

Today I feel we are fully capable of accepting expanded roles in the exploration of space.

In retrospect, we've all been particularly pleased with the call signs that we very laboriously chose for our spacecraft, Columbia and Eagle.

We've been particularly pleased with the emblem of our flight, depicting the U.S. eagle bringing the universal symbol of peace from the earth—from the planet earth—to the moon, that symbol being the olive branch.

It was our overall crew choice to deposit a replica of this symbol on the moon.

Personally, in reflecting on the events of the past several days, a verse from Psalms comes to mind to me:

When I consider Thy heavens, the work of Thy fingers, the moon and the stars, which Thou hast ordained, what is man that Thou art mindful of him?   *—Col. Edwin E. Aldrin Jr.*

The responsibility for this flight lies, first, with history, with giants of science who preceded this effort. Next, to the American people, who have, through their will, indicated desire. Next, the four administrations and their congresses for implementing that will.

And then, to the agency (NASA) and industry team that built our spacecraft, the Saturn, the Columbia, the Eagle, and the little EMU (extravehicular mobility unit), the space suit and backpack that was our small spacecraft out on the lunar surface.

We'd like to give a special thanks to all those Americans who built those spacecraft, who did the construction, design, the tests and put their hearts and all their abilities into those craft.
—Neil A. Armstrong, Mission Commander

Neil, Buzz and Mike, I want you to know that I think I'm the luckiest man in the world, and I say this not only because I have the honor to be President of the United States, but particularly because I have the privilege of speaking for so many in welcoming you back to earth.

I can tell you about all the messages we have received in Washington. Over 100 foreign governments, emperors and presidents and prime ministers and kings, have sent the most warm messages that we've ever received.

They represent over two billion people on this earth, all of them who have had the opportunity through television to see what you have done.

And then I also bring you messages from members of the Cabinet and members of the Senate and members of the House and the space agency. . . .

—*President Richard M. Nixon*

Following President Nixon's greeting, the chaplain of the *Hornet,* Lt. Cmdr. John A. Piirto, gave the following prayer:

Let us pray, Lord God, our Heavenly Father, our minds are staggered and our spirits exultant with the magnitude and precision of this entire Apollo 11 mission.

We have spent the past week in communal anxiety and hope as our astronauts sped through the glories and dangers of the heavens. As we try to understand and analyze the scope of this achievement for human life our reason is overwhelmed with abounding gratitude and joy, even as we realize the increasing challenges of the future.

This magnificent event illustrates anew what man can accomplish when purpose is firm and intent corporate.

A man on the moon was promised in this decade, and though some were unconvinced, the reality is with us this morning in the persons of Astronauts Armstrong, Aldrin and Collins.

We applaud their splendid exploits, and we pour out our thanksgiving for their safe return to us, to their families, to all mankind.

From our inmost beings we sing humble yet exuberant praise. May the great effort and commitment seen in this Project Apollo inspire our lives to move similarly in other areas of need.

May we, the people, by our enthusiasm and devotion and insight move to new landings in botherhood, human concern and mutual respect.

May our country, afire with inventive leadership and backed by a committed followership, blaze new trails into all areas of human cares.

See our enthusiasm and bless our joy with dedicated purpose for the many needs at hand. Link us in friendship with peoples throughout the world as we strive together to better the human condition. Grant us peace beginning in our hearts and a mind attuned with goodwill towards our neighbors.

All this we pray as our thanksgiving rings out to Thee in the name of Our Lord, Amen.

Voyage to the Moon

by Archibald MacLeish

PRESENCE among us,

      wanderer in our skies,

dazzle of silver in our leaves and on our
waters silver,

      O
silver evasion in our farthest thought—
"the visiting moon". . ."the glimpses of the moon". . .

and we have touched you!

      From the first of time,
before the first of time, before the
first men tasted time, we thought of you.
You were a wonder to us, unattainable,
a longing past the reach of longing,
a light beyond our light, our lives—perhaps
a meaning to us . . .

      Now
our hands have touched you in your depth of night.

Three days and three nights we journeyed,
steered by farthest stars, climbed outward,
crossed the invisible tide-rip where the floating dust
falls one way or the other in the void between,
followed that other down, encountered
cold, faced death—unfathomable emptiness . . .

Then, the fourth day evening, we descended,
made fast, set foot at dawn upon your beaches,
sifted between our fingers your cold sand.

We stand here in the dusk, the cold, the silence . . .

and here, as at the first of time, we lift our heads.
Over us, more beautiful than the moon, a
moon, a wonder to us, unattainable,
a longing past the reach of longing,
a light beyond our light, our lives—perhaps
a meaning to us . . .

      O, a meaning!

over us on these silent beaches the bright
earth,
      presence among us.

The Patriot

by Edgar A. Guest, from *The Friendly Way*
Copyright 1931 by The Reilly & Lee Company

The flag went by. He doffed his hat
And asked no praise for doing that;
He never boasted: "I am true!
I love the old Red, White and Blue!
I love my children and my wife;
Mine is a most unusual life,
Because it happens, don't you see,
I'm what I am supposed to be."

He paid his bills from week to week,
And never thought of them to speak;
He never seemed to be afraid
That men might think his debts unpaid;
He took for granted they would know
He lived as all good men below.
Thus quietly he went his way
Doing his work from day to day.

He never said: "Who looks at me
A law-abiding man will see."
When men by bars are not enclosed,
Respect for law is presupposed;
He could be trusted at his post
But never thought of that to boast,
And if you mentioned it, he'd say:
"A man's supposed to live that way."

He did his best, and let it go,
Without desire for pomp and show;
Those manly traits which marked him most
He never raised his voice to boast;
He played the neighbor; played the friend—
Was true to all men to the end,
And I should choose him from the lot
For what I'd call a patriot.

Intangible Blessings

by Rev. H. W. Burgan, D.D.

The earth, O Lord, is full of thy mercy.

Among the countless blessings which come to the human race from God there are at least four which can easily be overlooked even at Thanksgiving time.

The first is the miracle of memory. Memory for all of us can be a school of experience, and we sadly stand in need of such a school in a world like this. To remember our mistakes saves us many a moral pitfall; to forget plunges us into evils of every kind. On the other hand, it is the remembering helpful associates and inspiring moments that leads us to live ennobled lives.

Memory, too, makes the mind a treasure house. How enriched our lives are as we recall loved ones, delightful occasions, happy hours! In the midst of disappointments and tragedies we can have rightness and gladness in the thought of the cheering experiences of other days.

Not the least of memory's mercies is the capacity it affords us to understand and sympathize with our fellowmen. In given circumstances present with them, we can recall similar circumstances in which we have been placed. Out of the remembrance of these experiences we can put ourselves in their places and aid them in their distress.

* * * * *

The second blessing is the mercy of mystery. The meaning of things and events is to us largely incomprehensible. We cannot see the path ahead. We complain of the weary weight of uncertainty. The future is veiled. An ancient writer, however, declared, "It is the glory of God to conceal a thing." He believed that God's glory is vested in His wisdom and love for mankind in that He keeps the secrets of the future locked within Himself.

If the Pilgrim Fathers could have known before they left Delfhaven what was to be in store for them during that first dreadful winter in Plymouth, the Mayflower voyage would have been a very unhappy one for them, if indeed, it ever would have been undertaken. The power to see the future would have robbed our country of many a rich chapter in its unfolding history.

It is a mercy that we cannot see the future. We can be assured all the while of a Kindly Light that leads us through the encircling gloom.

* * * * *

The third providential endowment is the healing of time. A child cuts its thumb. A million invisible agents are at work to repair the damage. In time the hurt is cured. So with the human spirit. It is hurt. The year has taken its toll. But God patiently works through time to heal and save. In confidence and quietness, let us learn to wait.

* * * * *

The last benefaction is the fascination of change. We live in a world of altering scenes, customs and experiences—sea and land, day and night, heat and cold, childhood and old age, work and play, joy and sorrow. How dull would be a world without change! Even the shadows play their part in bringing welcome contrast. Take the shadows out of a landscape and what remains is flat and uninteresting. We would go stark mad if it were not for the variety in our experience.

A changing world disturbs us. God is not afraid of change. He has seen civilization rise and fall. In the midst of sweeping changes, let us listen for the voice of the Eternal, repent of our sins, acknowledge God in all our ways, and in the years ahead He will direct our steps.

* * * * *

Before the hills in order stood
Or earth received her fame,
From everlasting Thou are God,
The endless years the same.

Money Can Buy

A bed but not sleep.
Books but not brains.
Food but not appetite.
Finery but not beauty.
A house but not a home.
Medicine but not health.
Luxuries but not culture.
Amusement but not happiness.
Boon companions but not friends.
Flattery but not respect.

Great Spirit . . .

Grant that I may not criticize my
neighbor until I have walked a mile
in his moccasins.

"I Think Myself Well Off"

From Benjamin Franklin to his niece, Mrs. Partridge

Philadelphia, Nov. 25, 1788

My Dear Child: . . .

You kindly enquire after my health. I have not of late much reason to boast of it. People that will live a long life and drink to the bottom of the cup must expect to meet with some of the dregs. However, when I consider how many more terrible maladies the human body is liable to, I think myself well off that I have only three incurable ones—the gout, the stone, and old age; and, those notwithstanding, I enjoy many comfortable intervals, in which I forget all my ills and amuse myself in reading or writing, or in conversation with friends, joking, laughing, and telling merry stories, as when you first knew me, a young man about fifty. . . .

Your affectionate Uncle

Talk Happiness

by ELLA WHEELER WILCOX

Talk happiness. The world is sad enough
Without your woe. No path is wholly rough.
Look for the places that are smooth and clear,
And speak of them to rest the weary ear
Of earth, so hurt by one continuous strain
Of mortal discontent and grief and pain.

Talk faith. The world is better off without
Your uttered ignorance and morbid doubt.
If you have faith in God, or man, or self,
Say so; if not, push back upon the shelf
Of silence all your thoughts till faith shall come,
No one will grieve because your lips are dumb.

Talk health. The dreary, never-ending tale
Of mortal maladies is worn and stale;
You cannot charm or interest or please
By harping on that minor chord, disease.
Say you are well, or all is well with you,
And God shall hear your words and make them true!

Wit and Wisdom of Elbert Hubbard

From *Elbert Hubbard of East Aurora* by Felix Shay
By permission of Wm. H. Wise & Co., Inc., publishers

Elbert Hubbard was a pamphleteer; he was also an epigrammatist. Into a single sentence he could pack a world of meaning. Because *The Philistine* was famous for its smart sayings, a few samples are set down here for your divertissement:

It's getting so that it is harder to find a gentleman than a genius.

It's a wise guy who does not monkey with his destiny.

Hot air is all right, but see that it is well compressed before you use it.

A college degree does not lessen the length of your ears; it only conceals it.

To civilize mankind: Make marriage difficult and divorce easy.

Writers seldom write the things they think. They simply write the things they think other folks think they think.

Now, owls are not really wise—they only look that way. The owl is a sort of college professor.

He who admits that he, himself, is a worm ought not to complain when he is trodden on.

"No man is a hero to his valet." Heroes never have valets. It is perfectly safe to say that ninety-nine men out of a hundred, in civilized countries, are opposed to war. We recognize that life is short and the night cometh. Leave us alone!

I doubt much that the time will ever come when two pigs, meeting at the trough, will hesitate before jumping into the swill, and the bigger one say to the other, "After you, my dear Alphonse."

How sharper than a serpent's tooth is a thankless parent!

"You say," said the Reno Judge, "that your client was true to one woman?"
"Yes, your Honor; not only was he true to one woman, but more than that—he was true to five, as I can prove."

No man should be pitied except the one who wears his future for a bustle.

The greatest mistake you can make in this life is to be continually fearing you will make one.

You are what you think, and not what you think you are.

We can stop a Chinaman from coming to the United States; but we can not stop a Chinaman from going to Heaven! When we get across the River Styx, the first thing we will do is to go behind the ferry-house, and roar like cooing doves to think that we were born red and died bald and always took the thing so seriously.

Chickens always come home to roost, which is right and natural; but when they come to cackle and crow, that is another matter.

In parsing the word, "doormat," it is well to remember that it may be either male or female.

The author who has not made warm friends and then lost them in an hour by writing things that did not agree with the preconceived ideas of those friends, has either not written well or not been read.

You must not only bury your dead, but you must forget where, smoothing every grave—else you are not safe from ghosts—ghosts, my fine sir!

You can't get away from yourself by going to a booze-bazaar.

Don't sit down in the meadow and wait for the cow to back up and be milked—go after the cow.

Pushing to the front is very bad. You had better get in line and wait your turn, then you won't evolve a rhino spiritual rind and grow a crop of bristles up and down your back.

Women are all alike in this: they are all different, and most of them are different every hour.

To go fast, go slow.

* * * * *

"If you would be a successful publisher," said he, "get the best printing ink and the press built by Mr. Hoe that will print one million magazines a minute. The rest doesn't matter. Never mind about the literature: Mr. Munsey doesn't and he ought to know!" When one reads the careful, cautious, prudent, self-conscious cash-conscious twaddle that is passed out these days for "Editorial Opinion" one longs again for the fine free matter of Elbert Hubbard's "One-man magazine"—wherein Hubbard dared to embrace an Idea and an Ideal, dared to have an opinion—and dared to *lead* subscribers instead of cringing after them!

The Moss Covered Bucket that Hung on the Well

by Samuel Woodworth

How dear to my heart are the days of my childhood,
When fond recollection presents to my view
The orchard, the meadow, the deep tangled wildwood,
And every loved spot which my infancy knew;
The wide spreading pond, and the mill which stood near it;
The bridge and the rock where the cataract fell,
The cot of my father, the dairy-house near it,
And e'en the rude bucket that hung on the well—
   The old oaken bucket,
   The iron bound bucket,
The moss covered bucket that hung on the well.

That moss covered bucket I hail as a treasure;
For often at noon, when returned from the field,
I found it the source of an exquisite pleasure,
The purest and sweetest that nature could yield.
How ardent I seized, with hands that were glowing,
And quick to the white pebbled bottom it fell;
Then soon, with the emblem of truth overflowing,
And dripping with coolness, it rose from the well.
   The old oaken bucket,
   The iron bound bucket,
The moss covered bucket arose from the well.

How sweet from the green mossy rim to receive it,
As poised on the curb it inclined to my lips;
Not a full flowing goblet could tempt me to leave it,
Though filled with the nectar that Jupiter sips.
And now, far removed from that situation,
The tear of regret will intrusively swell,
As fancy reverts to my father's plantation;
And sighs for the bucket which hung on the well.
   The old oaken bucket,
   The iron bound bucket,
The moss covered bucket that hung on the well.

· 25 ·

Just Money Never Made Friends with Anybody

*Reactions encountered by a self-made diplomat, Will Rogers,
during a trip abroad, as reported in a letter to President
Calvin Coolidge from Cork, Ireland, August 26, 1926.*

Reprinted with permission of Albert and Charles Boni, Inc.

You don't know how many people in every country are pulling
for a revolution. The outs always think that that will give them
a chance to get in. So you see, it is harder to overcome wars than
you would at first think. Of course, this is not an argument to
say that you shouldn't try. For why they want to fight is more
than I will ever know. Now this trouble over here about these
debts, that goes further back than the debts.

The main thing is a misunderstanding about the amount we did
in the war. It is a favorite topic over here to belittle what we did
in the war, and we think we helped them out quite a bit; and it is
over that that the trouble is, and not over a few millions of Pounds
or Francs. If we thought that they really at heart and conscien-
tiously appreciated what we did in the war, I think there would
be no trouble to get the debt canceled in full. But they at heart
don't seem to think we did very much, so there the real trouble lies.
There is just a misunderstanding about the real value of America's
services in the war. It has been quite a good while since they were
saved, and they are not willing to admit that they were saved. Just
money never made friends with anybody. If a few millions of dollars is going to part our friendship, why, the friendship was never
very deep. America feels they are not out buying people's friendship. If they can't do it by associating with them, and helping them
in a common cause and going through a war with them, why, presenting them with a few million is not going to help us out.

You hear a lot about doing things to foster good relations
between nations. The worst thing and the worst word that came
out of the entire war was "propaganda." Propaganda means doing
something for a reason; or, in other words, acting a part for a
cause. Well, if we can't act natural and have people like us for
what we really are, why, all the propaganda in the world will do
no good. Propaganda is the easiest thing in the world detected,
and the nation or individual that you are trying it on is the first
to detect it.

There is nothing in the world that makes an individual so mad
as to know that someone is trying to do some certain thing to
curry favor with him, and it is the same with Nations.

Let a Nation do like an individual—that is, I mean a real individual. Let 'em go through life and do and act like they want to, and if they can't gain friends on their own accounts, don't let's go out and try and buy it. Any time you go out purposely to make friends with someone, the result is generally terrible. It's this trying to stand in that has got us where we are. If we would stay at home and quit trying to prowl around to various conferences and conventions somewhere, we would be better off.

We, unfortunately, don't make a good impression collectively. You see a bunch of Americans at anything abroad and they generally make more noise and have more to say than anybody, and generally create a worse impression than if they had stayed at home. They are throwing rocks at us, but sometimes you think it is deserved. There should be a law prohibiting over three Americans going anywhere abroad together.

But here is what I want you to get clear, Cal, when they talk about us being in so bad: Say, we haven't started to get in bad. Some of these Nations have been hating each other for generations, while they are only just starting in hating us. Some of them can't hate us so much, because we have never fought against them in their lives and have never taken any land away from them. So when it comes to being in wrong in Europe we are only an Amateur.

To Have a Friend—Be One

The only way to have a friend
    Is to be one yourself;
The only way to keep a friend
    Is to give from that wealth.

For friendship must be doublefold,
    Each one must give his share
Of feelings true if he would reap
    The blessings that are there.

If you would say, "He is my friend,"
    Then nothing else will do
But you must say, "I am his friend,"
    And prove that fact be true!

                         –*J. B. D.*

Grumble Corner and Thanksgiving Street

I knew a man whose name was Horner,
Who used to live on Grumble Corner;
Grumble Corner, in Cross-Patch Town,
He was never seen without a frown.
He grumbled at this; he grumbled at that;
He growled at the dog; he growed at the cat;
He grumbled at morning; he grumbled at night;
And to grumble and growl were his chief delight.

One day, as I loitered along the street,
My old acquaintance I chanced to meet;
His face was without the look of care
And the ugly frown that it used to wear.
"I may be mistaken, perhaps," I said,
As, after saluting, I turned my head;
"But it is, and it isn't, the Mr. Horner
Who lived so long on Grumble Corner!"

I met him next day; and I met him again
In melting weather, in pouring rain;
When stocks were up and when stocks were down;
But a smile somehow had replaced the frown.
It puzzled me much, and so, one day,
I seized his hand in a friendly way
And said, "Mr. Horner, I'd like to know
What has happened to change you so?"

He laughed a laugh that was good to hear,
For it told of a conscience calm and clear;
And he said, with none of the old-time drawl,
"Why, I've changed my residence, that is all!"
"Changed your residence?" "Yes," said Horner,
"It wasn't healthy on Grumble Corner,
And so I moved; 'twas a change complete;
And you'll find me now on Thanksgiving Street."

Now every day as I move along
The streets so filled with the busy throng,
I watch each face, and can always tell
Where men and women and children dwell.
And many a discontented mourner
Is spending his days on Grumble Corner,
Sour and sad, whom I long to entreat
To take a house on Thanksgiving Street.

—*Author unknown*

Perhaps It Is We Who Are Savages!

From a very rare volume printed in 1735 entitled
New Voyages to North America *by the Baron Lahontan,*
Lord-Lieutenant of the French Colony at Placentia in Newfoundland

The savages [North American Indians] are utter strangers to distinctions of property, for what belongs to one is equally another's. If any one of them be in danger at the beaver hunting, the rest fly to his assistance, without being so much as asked. If his fusee [gun] bursts, they are ready to offer him their own. If any of his children be killed, or taken by the enemy, he is presently furnished with as many slaves as he hath occasion for.

Money is in use with none of them but [except] those that are Christians, who live in the suburbs of our towns. The others will not touch or so much as look upon silver, but give it the odious name of the *French Serpent.*

They'll tell you that amongst us the people murder, plunder, defame, and betray one another for money—that the husbands make merchandise of their wives, and the mothers of their daughters, for the lucre of that metal. They think it unaccountable that one man should have more than another, and that the rich should have more respect than the poor. In short, they say the name of savages, which we bestow upon them, would fit ourselves better, since there is nothing in our actions that bears an appearance of wisdom.

Such as have been in France were continually teasing us with the faults and disorders they observed in our towns as being occasioned by money. 'Tis in vain to remonstrate to them how useful the distinction of property is for the support of a society. They make a jest of what's to be said on that head.

In fine [truth], they neither quarrel nor fight, nor slander one another. They scoff at arts and sciences, and laugh at the difference of degrees which is observed with us. They brand us for slaves, and call us miserable souls whose life is not worth having, alleging that we degrade ourselves in subjecting ourselves to one man who possesses the whole power and is bound by no law but his own will—that we have continual jars [arguments] among ourselves—that our children rebel against their parents—that we imprison one another and publicly promote our own destruction.

Besides, they value themselves above anything that you can imagine, and this is the reason they always give for it—that one's as much master as another, and since men are all made of the same clay, there should be no distinction or superiority among them.

They pretend that their contented way of living far surpasses our riches, that all our sciences are not so valuable as the art of leading a peaceful, calm life, and that a man is not a man with us any farther than riches will make him; but among them the true qualifications of a man are—

> To run well—to hunt—to bend the bow—to manage the fusee—to work a canoe—to understand war—to know forests—to subsist upon a little—to build cottages—to fell trees—to be able to travel a hundred leagues in a wood without any guide or other provision than his bow and arrows.

They say we are great cheats in selling them bad wares four times dearer than they are worth, by way of exchange for their beaver-skins, and that our fusees are continually bursting and laming them, after they have paid sufficient prices for them.

I wish I had time to recount the innumerable absurdities they are guilty of relating to our customs, but to be particular upon that head would be a work of ten or twelve days.

Fate

by BRET HARTE

"The sky is clouded, the rocks are bare;
The spray of the tempest is white in air;
The winds are out with the waves at play,
And I shall not tempt the sea today.

"The trail is narrow, the wood is dim,
The panther clings to the arching limb;
And the lion's whelps are abroad at play,
And I shall not join in the chase today."

But the ship sailed safely over the sea,
And the hunters came from the chase in glee;
And the town that was builded upon a rock
Was swallowed up in the earthquake shock.

Ode to Haverhill Academy
on the occasion of its dedication in 1827
by John Greenleaf Whittier

An expression that is startlingly appropriate to the successful completion of the Journey to the Moon

Hail, Star of Science! Come forth in thy splendor,
  Illumine these walls—let them evermore be
A shrine where thy votaries offerings may tender,
  Hallowed by genius, and sacred to thee.
    Warmed by thy genial glow,
    Here let thy laurels grow
Greenly for those who rejoice at thy name.
    Here let thy spirit rest,
    Thrilling the ardent breast,
Rousing the soul with thy promise of fame.

Companion of Freedom! The light of her story,
  Wherever her voice at thine altar is known
There shall no cloud of oppression come o'er thee,
  No envious tyrant thy splendor disown.
    Sons of the proud and free
    Joyous shall cherish thee,
Long as their banners in triumph shall wave;
    And from its peerless height
    Ne'er shall thy orb of light
Sink, but to set upon Liberty's grave.

Smile then upon us; on hearts that have never
  Bowed down 'neath oppression's unhallowed control.
Spirit of Science! O, crown our endeavor;
  Here shed thy beams on the night of the soul;
    Then shall thy sons entwine,
    Here for thy sacred shrine,
Wreaths that shall flourish through ages to come,
    Bright in thy temple seen,
    Robed in immortal green,
Fadeless memorials of genius shall bloom.

Three Words of Strength

by FRIEDRICH VON SCHILLER

There are three lessons I would write—
Three words, as with a burning pen,
In tracings of eternal light—
Upon the hearts of men.

Have Hope. Though clouds environ round,
And gladness hides her face in scorn,
Put off the shadow from thy brow—
No night but hath its morn.

Have Faith. Where'er thy bark is driven—
The calm's disport, the tempest's mirth—
Know this: God rules the host of Heaven,
The inhabitants of earth.

Have Love. Not love alone for one;
But man, as man, thy brother call;
And scatter, like the circling sun,
Thy charities on all.

Thus grave these lessons on thy soul—
Hope, Faith, and Love and thou shalt find
Strength when life's surges rudest roll,
Light when thou else wert blind.

Recipe for a Happy Day

by ARTHUR LEWIS TUBBS

A heart full of thankfulness,
A thimbleful of care;
A soul of simple hopefulness,
An early morning prayer;
A smile to greet the morning with,
A kind word as a key
To ope the door and greet the day,
Whate'er it brings to thee.
A patient trust in Providence
To sweeten all the way—
All these, combined with thoughtfulness,
Will make a happy day.

Wisdom Can Be Taught

From *Plato's Best Thoughts*

Let us consider this further point, I said: Seeing that all men desire happiness, and happiness, as has been shown, is gained by a use, and a right use, of the things of life, and the right use of them, and good fortune in the use of them, is given by knowledge, the inference is that every man ought by all means to try and make himself as wise as he can?

Yes, he said.

And the desire to obtain this treasure, which is far more precious than money, from a father or a guardian or a friend or a suitor, whether citizen or stranger— the eager desire and prayer to them that they would impart wisdom to you, is not at all dishonorable, Cleinias; nor is any one to be blamed for doing any honorable service or ministration to any man, whether a lover or not, if his aim is to get wisdom. Do you agree to that? I said.

Yes, he said, I quite agree, and think that you are right.

Yes, I said, Cleinias, if only wisdom can be taught, and does not come to man spontaneously; for that is a point which has still to be considered, and is not yet agreed upon by you and me.

But I think, Socrates, that wisdom can be taught, he said.

Best of men, I said, I am delighted to hear you say that; and I am also grateful to you for having saved me from a long and tiresome speculation as to whether wisdom can be taught or not. But now, as you think that wisdom can be taught, and that wisdom only can make a man happy and fortunate, will you not acknowledge that all of us ought to love wisdom, and you individually will try to love her?

Certainly, Socrates, he said; and I will do my best.

❊❊❊❊❊❊❊

The Importance of Being Willing to Learn

From *The Children's Bible, Selections from the Old and New Testaments*
translated and arranged by Henry A. Sherman and Charles Foster Kent.
Copyright, 1922, by Charles Scribner's Sons

The lips of the wise speak knowledge,
But the fool does not understand.
A fool's way seems right in his sight,
But a wise man listens to advice.
A fool despises his father's correction,
But he who regards reproof acts wisely.

Listen to advice and receive instruction,
That you may be wise in your later life.
Advice in a man's mind is like deep water,
But a man of sense will draw it out.
Hold fast instruction, let it not go;
Keep it, for it is your life.

My son, reject not the discipline of the Lord,
And do not spurn his reproof,
For whom he loves he reproves,
Even as a father the son of whom he is fond.
He who rejects correction despises his own self,
But he who listens to reproof gains understandi

Phizzog

by CARL SANDBURG

From *Good Morning, America*, copyright 1928, 1956 by CARL S
Reprinted by permission of Harcourt, Brace & World, I

This face you got,
This here phizzog you carry around,
You never picked it out for yourself,
    at all, at all—did you?
This here phizzog—somebody handed it
    to you—am I right?
Somebody said, "Here's yours, now go see
    what you can do with it."
Somebody slipped it to you and it was like
    a package marked:
"No goods exchanged after being taken away"—
This face you got.

· 35 ·

Time

Little ones think it's eternity;
The days before Christmas are endless;
The two-hour nap seems insanity,
And time is slow-paced and relentless.

Then comes school, with its rules so precise,
And time starts to run in reverse.
A twenty-minute recess melts like ice,
While a one-hour class drags on like a hearse.

Joyful summers, free from strife,
And light-hearted Christmases gaily pass,
Till the bell that governs school-day life
Finally rings for my very last class.

That old devil time arises again—
Time to look for a job and start to work,
Time to travel; there's much to gain.
The whole world beckons—I must not shirk.

And then, all at once I am twenty-one,
With plenty of time for everything!
A time for work and a time for fun—
A time to laugh and a time to sing.

The happy hours and days fly past;
The seasons change, the months slip by,
Till all of a sudden it's time, at last,
To walk down the aisle with that favorite guy.

So true it is, as the poet has said,
"There is a time for everything."
A time to rejoice, a time to be sad,
But today is a time to laugh and sing.

—J. C. J.

Medical Practices Two Hundred Years Ago

From *The North American's Almanack for 1776* by SAMUEL STEARNS
Directions for preserving the health of the soldiers in the camps

When the weather is cold and the air is pure and dry, if the soldiers are well clothed, there are but a few diseases produced; but when the weather is unsettled, cloudy, wet and rainy, the usual consequences are colds attended with feverish inflammatory symptoms, especially rheumatic, pleuritic and peripneumonic complaints, and if proper means are neglected they will soon generate into consumptions, or chronic rheumatisms, and so forth.

When soldiers undergo an uncommon degree of fatigue and are much chilled with the cold in wet, damp weather, they should drink often of the following mixture, namely—To one quart of small beer, add half a pint of brandy, sweetened with molasses, which mixture may be acidulated with a little vinegar or cream of tartar to render palatable.

Soldiers should never sleep in wet clothes, nor on the wet ground. Keep the stomach warm in cold weather, and the breast, kidneys, in free from obstructions, it will be proper to drink a small dram of garlic and brandy, but this or no other dram should o a soldier who is almost chilled to death with the cold, for it has often proved fatal. He should be immediately put bed and have some warm gruel or sage tea given him, may be allowed a dram. When a soldier is obliged to be ather, he should use exercise to keep his blood in a nd prevent it from being chilled with the cold.

d greens should often be allowed to the soldiers in ir living a long time upon salt provision proves eir health. An army should therefore be supplied od roots, fruits and vegetables, such as onions, ps, parsnips, carrots, cabbage, apples, pears, lums, soft fresh bread, cider, lemons, oranges, mon herbs that are proper in season, such as ress, sharp pointed dock, brook lime, and the like utics, which would be a light refreshment for

many diseases owe their origin to poisonous exhala- nd in this class are acute fevers with exanthemata as the small pox, measles, tertians, quartans, double fevers, pleurisies, opthalmias, quinsies, catarrhal benign as malignant, erysipelatious disorders, rheuma- arrheas, dysenteries, bastard pleurisies, and so forth.

It will be proper for soldiers in hot weather to drink punch that is well acidulated with the juice of lemons and oranges, or if these cannot be had, the cream of tartar will answer. It has been observed that the juice of lemons is a great antidote against malignant fevers, it having a tendency to prevent the corruption of the animal fluids. Punch that is made of rum and sugar with the cream of tartar is a very salutary composition, which is of a cooling, strengthening, antiputrid and diuretic nature, and will greatly repress all inflammatory diseases.

A soldier should never lay himself down to sleep immediately after he has done supper, but should use some sort of exercise to promote digestion, and if his digestion is weak he may chew rhubarb, which will strengthen it wonderfully.

He should keep himself as clean as possible, for those that wear dirty clothing and live an idle, sedentary life and feed chiefly upon salt meat, old dry biscuit, sarinaceous vegetables, peas, beans and old cheese, and so forth, are very subject to many dangerous diseases and especially the scurvy, which is known by a spontaneous weariness and heaviness of the body, a difficulty of breathing after bodily exercise, a rottenness of the gums, and a stinking breath, a frequent bleeding at the nose, difficulty of walking, a swelling or falling away of the legs, with livid, plumbeous yellow or violet colored spots, and the color of the face is often pale and tawny. Those that are afflicted with the disease should adhere to a proper regimen which consists of fresh meat-broths, greens or vegetables with the juice of oranges and lemons.

A recipe for the cure of the dysentery or camp distemper

Take bayberry wax, loaf sugar and mutton tallow, of each an ounce. Boil them all together in three pints of skim milk. When it is cooled take a teacup full once every hour.

Wintertime

When the cold wind blows,
Take care of your nose
That it doesn't get froze,
And wrap up your toes
In warm woolen hose.
The above we suppose
Was written in prose,
By someone who knows
The effect of cold snows.

Christmas Bells

by HENRY WADSWORTH LONGFELLOW

I heard the bells on Christmas Day
Their old, familiar carols play,
    And wild and sweet
    The words repeat
Of peace on earth, good will to men!

And thought how, as the day had come,
The belfries of all Christendom
    Had rolled along
    The unbroken song
Of peace on earth, good will to men!

Till, ringing, singing on its way,
The world revolved from night to day,
    A voice, a chime,
    A chant sublime
Of peace on earth, good will to men!

Then from each black, accursed mouth
The cannon thundered in the South,
    And with the sound
    The carols drowned
Of peace on earth, good will to men!

It was as if an earthquake rent
The hearthstones of a continent,
    And made forlorn
    The households born
Of peace on earth, good will to men!

And in despair I bowed my head;
"There is no peace on earth," I said,
    "For hate is strong,
    And mocks the song
Of peace on earth, good will to men!"

Then pealed the bells more loud and deep:
"God is not dead, nor doth He sleep!
    The Wrong shall fail,
    The Right prevail,
With peace on earth, good will to men!"

Lincoln's Influence — Upon His Contemporaries and Succeeding Generations — Spanned Decades

by JANE ADDAMS, from *Twenty Years at Hull House*

I suppose all the children who were born about the time of the Civil War have recollections quite unlike those of the children who are living now. Although I was but four and a half years old when Lincoln died, I distinctly remember the day when I found on our two white gate posts American flags companioned with black. I tumbled down on the harsh gravel walk in my eager rush into the house to inquire what they were "there for." To my amazement I found my father in tears, something that I had never seen before, having assumed, as all children do, that grown-up people never cried. The two flags, my father's tears and his impressive statement that the greatest man in the world had died, constituted my initiation, my baptism, as it were, into the thrilling and solemn interests of a world lying quite outside the two white gate posts.

The great war touched children in many ways: I remember an engraved roster of names, headed by the words "Addams' Guard," and the whole surmounted by the insignia of the American eagle clutching many flags, which always hung in the family living-room. As children we used to read this list of names again and again. We could reach it only by dint of putting the family Bible on a chair and piling the dictionary on top of it; using the Bible to stand on was always accompanied by a little thrill of superstitious awe, although we carefully put the dictionary above that our profane feet might touch it alone.

Having brought the roster within reach of our eager fingers,— fortunately it was glazed,— we would pick out the names of those who "had fallen on the field" from those who "had come back from the war," and from among the latter those whose children were our schoolmates. When drives were planned, we would say, "Let us take this road," that we might pass the farm where a soldier had once lived; if flowers from the garden were to be given away, we would want them to go to the mother of one of those heroes whose names we knew from the "Addams' Guard." If a guest should become interested in the roster on the wall, he was at once led by the eager children to a small picture of Colonel Davis which hung next the opposite window, that he might see the brave Colonel of the Regiment.

*   *   *

My father always spoke of the martyred President as Mr. Lincoln, and I never heard the great name without a thrill. I remember the

*President Lincoln and his son, Tad, on April 9, 1865,
five days before the assassination of Lincoln.*

day—it must have been one of comparative leisure, perhaps a Sunday
—when at my request my father took out of his desk a thin packet
marked "Mr. Lincoln's Letters," the shortest one of which bore
unmistakable traces of that remarkable personality. These letters
began, "My dear Double-D'ed Addams," and to the inquiry as to
how the person thus addressed was about to vote on a certain measure

then before the legislature, was added the assurance that he knew that this Addams "would vote according to his conscience," but he begged to know in which direction the same conscience "was pointing." As my father folded up the bits of paper I fairly held my breath in my desire that he should go on with the reminiscence of this wonderful man, whom he had known in his comparative obscurity, or better still, that he should be moved to tell some of the exciting incidents of the Lincoln-Douglas debates.

There were at least two pictures of Lincoln that always hung in my father's room, and one in our old-fashioned upstairs parlor, of Lincoln with little Tad. For one or all of these reasons I always tend to associate Lincoln with the tenderest thoughts of my father.

I recall a time of great perplexity in the summer of 1894, when Chicago was filled with federal troops sent there by the President of the United States, and their presence was resented by the governor of the state, that I walked the wearisome way from Hull-House to Lincoln Park—for no cars were running regularly at that moment of sympathetic strikes—in order to look at and gain magnanimous counsel, if I might, from the marvelous St. Gaudens statue which had been but recently placed at the entrance of the park. Some of Lincoln's immortal words were cut into the stone at his feet, and never did a distracted town more sorely need the healing of "with charity towards all" than did Chicago at that moment, and the tolerance of the man who had won charity for those on both sides of "an irrepressible conflict."

*   *   *

Of the many old friends of my father who kindly came to look up his daughter in the first days of Hull-House, I recall none with more pleasure than Lyman Trumbull, whom we used to point out to the members of the Young Citizens' Club as the man who had for days held in his keeping the Proclamation of Emancipation until his friend President Lincoln was ready to issue it. I remember the talk he gave at Hull-House on one of our early celebrations of Lincoln's birthday, his assertion that Lincoln was no cheap popular hero, that the "common people" would have to make an effort if they would understand his greatness, as Lincoln painstakingly made a long effort to understand the greatness of the people.

There was something in the admiration of Lincoln's contemporaries, or at least of those men who had known him personally, which was quite unlike even the best of the devotion and reverent understanding which has developed since. In the first place, they had so large a fund of common experience; they too had pioneered in a western country, and had urged the development of canals and railroads in order that the raw prairie crops might be transported to market; they too had realized that if this last tremendous experiment in self-government failed here, it would be the disappointment of the centuries and that upon their ability to organize self-government in state, county and town depended the verdict of history. These men also knew, as Lincoln himself did, that if this tremendous experiment was to come to fruition, it must be brought about by the people themselves; that there was no other capital fund upon which to draw.

*   *   *

In our early effort at Hull-House to hand on to our neighbors whatever of help we had found for ourselves, we made much of Lincoln. We were often distressed by the children of immigrant parents who were ashamed of the pit whence they were dug, who repudiated the language and customs of their elders, and counted themselves successful as they were able to ignore the past. Whenever I held up Lincoln for their admiration as the greatest American, I invariably pointed out his marvelous power to retain and utilize past experiences; that he never forgot how the plain people in Sangamon County thought and felt when he himself had moved to town; that this habit was the foundation for his marvelous capacity for growth; that during those distracting years in Washington it enabled him to make clear beyond denial to the American people themselves, the goal towards which they were moving. I was sometimes bold enough to add that proficiency in the art of recognition and comprehension did not come without effort, and that certainly its attainment was necessary for any successful career in our conglomerate America.

*   *   *

Is it not Abraham Lincoln who has cleared the title to our democracy? He made plain, once for all, that democratic government, associated as it is with all the mistakes and shortcomings of the common people, still remains the most valuable contribution America has made to the moral life of the world.

Speech and Silence

by Bliss Carman and Richard Hovey

The words that pass from lip to lip
For souls still out of reach!
A friend for that companionship
That's deeper than all speech!

· 45 ·

A Morning Visitant

by W. W. Argow

A new unblemished Day has come to me out of the city of eternity. Carelessly Today unfolds its gathered treasures and bids me choose my heart's desires. So I have chosen that without which I would be poorer and others impoverished because of me.

A simple faith in the goodness of men, and their faith in me; believing that they try as sincerely to follow the gleam as I.

A sustaining trust in the nearness of health, the immediacy of joy, the constancy of happiness, the sufficiency of strength.

A fleeting glimpse of beauty wreathing a child's face, glowing in a poem, or hidden in something which the hand of man has made.

A worthy work that taxes my strength, tests my patience and redeems my life from a meaningless existence.

A daring love that counts no costs, exacts no sureties, reckons no rewards; but in its glad abandon gives itself to the uttermost.

A few leisure moments for wonder to envelop me, that mystery may touch the sensitive cords of my soul.

And so when Today kisses me good night I shall know that it was God who came to me.

To Age

by Walter Savage Landor

Welcome, old friend! These many years
   Have we lived door by door;
The Fates have laid aside their shears
   Perhaps for some few more.

I was indocile at an age
   When better boys were taught,
But thou at length hast made me sage,
   If I am sage in aught.

Little I know from other men,
   Too little they from me,
But thou hast pointed well the pen
   That writes these lines to thee.

Thanks for expelling Fear and Hope,
  One vile, the other vain;
One's scourge, the other's telescope,
  I shall not see again;

Rather what lies before my feet
  My notice shall engage:
He who hath braved Youth's dizzy heat
  Dreads not the frost of Age.

Youth Is a State of Mind
by ROBERT FRÓTHINGHAM, from *Youth*

Youth is not a time of life; it is a state of mind. It is not a matter of ripe cheeks, red lips and supple knees; it is a temper of the will, a quality of the imagination, a vigor of the emotions. It is the freshness of the deep springs of life.

Youth means a temperamental predominance of courage over timidity, of the appetite for adventure over the love of ease. This often exists in a man of fifty more than in a boy of twenty.

Nobody grows old by merely living a number of years. People grow old only by deserting their ideals.

Years wrinkle the skin; but to give up your enthusiasm wrinkles the soul.

Worry, doubt, self-distrust, fear and despair—these are the long, long years that bow the head and turn the flaming spirit back to dust.

You are as young as your faith, as old as your doubt; as young as your self-confidence, as old as your fear; as young as your hope, as old as your despair.

In the central place of your heart is an evergreen tree; its name is Love. So long as it flourishes you are young. When it dies you are old. In the central place of your heart is a wireless station; so long as it receives messages of beauty, hope, cheer, grandeur, courage and power from God and your fellow men, so long are you young.

But dost thou love life? Then do not squander time, for that is the stuff that life is made of!

Human felicity is produced not so much by great pieces of fortune that seldom happen as by little advantages that happen every day.
—*Benjamin Franklin*

Recognize the Virtues

From *Cheerio's Book of Days* by Charles K. Field
Copyright, 1940, by Garden City Publishing Co., Inc.

(He called it "Vocational Friendship.")

Vocational experts examine candidates and determine the particular vocation for which each is best adapted. One man may be poor at bookkeeping but can drive a car well. Just so with my friends I try to find the function each can best exercise in our relationship. One friend may be a charming conversationalist but is always late to appointments. So I enjoy his talk always, but I never make engagements with him. Another may have exquisite table manners but she talks, talks while we are at a play. So I invite her to dinners, but never to the theatre.

The thing is to find these points of sympathetic contact with each friend, and avoid other points. I don't expect a friend always to please my particular taste, nor do I expect always to please him. Friends are like tools. A saw is used for cutting and you mustn't expect it to be a screw driver. So friends should be used for the parts they play best. We are too apt to expect our friends to come up to our standard in every respect, to be able to do anything, like those knives boys love with twenty-four blades and tools all in one handle.

Every person has some splendid traits and if we confine our contacts so as to bring those traits into action, there is no need of ever being bored or irritated or indignant. (I knew a girl once and the only thing she could do agreeably to me was to laugh. So I always kept her laughing and she is still my good friend.) I assure you this is a practical working theory of friendship and if you believe it and practice it, you may truly say that every one is, potentially, your friend.

Secrets

by BLISS CARMAN and RICHARD HOVEY

Three secrets that never were said:
The stir of the sap in the spring,
The desire of a man to a maid,
The urge of a poet to sing.

"Contented industry is the mainspring of human happiness."

A quotation from a letter written by Dr. William J. Mayo of the Mayo Clinic in Rochester, Minnesota, to the University of Minnesota in 1934

As a man advances in years, he begins to look backward over those conditions and happenings in the past that influenced his life work. To grow up in a doctor's family with a professional background of some generations will likely have, as it did with my brother and myself, that sort of influence which leads not to conscious choice of medicine as a career, but rather to unconscious elimination of every other choice. Neither my brother nor I ever had an idea of being anything but a doctor.

Our father recognized certain definite social obligations. He believed that any man who had better opportunity than others, greater strength of mind, body or character, owed something to those who had not been so provided; that is, that the important thing in life is not to accomplish for one's self alone, but for each to carry his share of collective responsibility. Stepping as we did into a large general practice, with a great deal of surgery from the beginning, my brother and I had an exceptional opportunity, and as we entered medical practice during the early period of the development of asepsis and antisepsis in surgery, which had come through the work of Pasteur and Lister, this opportunity was unique. We were especially fortunate that we had the benefit of our father's large experience to help us to apply the modern methods to replace the old type of surgery which up to that time had been practiced. There being two of us, with absolute mutual confidence, each of us was able to travel at home and abroad each year for definite periods of study of subjects connected with surgery, as well as to attend medical meetings, while the other was at home carrying on the practice.

In 1894, having paid for our homes and started a modest life insurance program, we decided upon a plan whereby we could eventually do something worthwhile for the sick. This plan was to put aside from our earnings any sums in excess of what might be called a reasonable return for the work we accomplished. It seemed to us then, as now, that moneys which should accumulate over and above the amount necessary for a living, under circumstances which would give favorable conditions to work and to prepare reasonably for our families, would interfere seriously with the object that we had in view.

Contented industry is the mainspring of human happiness.

Money is so likely to encourage waste of time, changing of objectives in life, living under circumstances which put one out of touch with those who have been lifelong friends, who perhaps have been less fortunate. How many families have been ruined by money which has taken away from younger members the desire to labor and achieve and has introduced elements into their lives whereby, instead of being useful citizens, they have become wasteful and sometimes profligate.

*　　*　　*　　*　　*

All questions in this country can be and should be settled by the ballot box, and in the long run, rightly. As long as public questions are decided without passion or violence by the ballot box, our country and our institutions are safe.

—Dr. William J. Mayo

Do One Thing at a Time and Do It Well

From *The Day-Book of John Stuart Blackie*

I

My rule of life is with sure plan to work,
　To trust in God and sing a cheerful song;
To search what gem in each cold day may lurk,
　And catch a side-advantage from a wrong.

II

Not what you plan alone, and what you do,
　But when and where, how much, and how you
　　do it;
These rule the chanceful games of life, and you
　Must wisely view each move, or you will rue it.

III

Wouldst thou lead a happy life?
　Believe the thing that's said, boy;
By the handle take the knife,
　And never by the blade, boy.

And if aught may chance amiss,
　At home or in the street, boy,
Seek—and you will find—a kiss
　In every cross you meet, boy.

IV

Have no faith in what thou fearest,
　　Evil finds who evil fears;
And for vanished loves the dearest
　　Weep, but never nurse your tears.

Watch and wait, look not for wonders,
　　Scan the time with watchful eyes;
Let the past's distressful blunders
　　Teach the future to be wise.

V

With wisdom plan and with stout patience plod,
And leave the growth of well-sown seed to God.

VI

Never hurry, never worry,
　　Never fret and fume,
And when the Devil shows his face,
　　Bid him leave the room.

VII

Don't be hasty, and don't be slack,
And always keep a reserve at your back.

VIII

How make your wit and your width to swell?
Do one thing at a time, and do it well.

◆◆◆◆◆

Expert Advice
by JOSH BILLINGS

As in a game of cards, so in the game of life we must play what is dealt out to us; and the glory consists not so much in winning as in playing a poor hand well.

And if you ever find happiness by hunting for it, you will find it, as the old woman did her lost spectacles, safe on her own nose all the time!

And remember this: every time a man laughs he takes a kink out of the chain of life. For laughing is the sensation of feeling good all over but showing it particularly in one spot.

When the Devil Was Sick
Could He Prove It?

by OGDEN NASH, from *Verses From 1929 On*
Copyright 1940 by The Curtis Publishing Co.
Published by Little, Brown and Company

Few things are duller
Than feeling unspecifically off-color,
Yes, you feel like the fulfillment of a dismal prophecy,
And you don't feel either exercisey or officey,
But still you can't produce a red throat or a white tongue or
uneasy respiration or any kind of a symptom,
And it is very embarrassing that whoever was supposed to be
passing out the symptoms skymptom,
Because whatever is the matter with you, you can't spot it
But whatever it is, you've got it,
But the question is how to prove it,

And you suck for hours on the mercury of the thermometer you
　　finally sent out for and you can't move it,
And your entire system may be pneumococci'd or streptococci'd,
But the looks you get from your loved ones are simply skepti-
　　cocci'd,
And Conscience glares at you in her Here comes that bad penny
　　way,
Crying There's nothing the matter with you, you're just trying
　　to get out of doing something you never wanted to do
　　anyway,
So you unfinger your pulse before Conscience can jeer at you for
　　a fingerer,
And you begin to believe that perhaps she is right, perhaps you
　　are nothing but a hypochondriacal old malingerer,
And you take a farewell look at the thermometer,
And that's when you hurl the bometer.
Yes sir, it's as good as a tonic,
Because you've got as pretty a ninety-nine point one as you'd
　　wish to see in a month of bubonic.
Some people hold out for a hundred or more before they collapse
But that leaves too many gaps;
As for me,
I can get a very smug Monday, Tuesday, Wednesday, Thursday,
　　or Friday in bed out of a tenth of a degree.
It is to this trait that I am debtor
For the happy fact that on week ends I generally feel better.

When a man is laboring under the pain of any distemper,
it is then that he recollects there is a God, and that he
himself is but a man.

　　　　　　　　　　　　　　　　　　—*Pliny the Elder*

I enjoy convalescence. It is the part that makes the illness
worth while.

　　　　　　　　　　　　　　　　　—*George Bernard Shaw*

Life's a Game — Don't Flinch — Play the Game!
by Theodore Roosevelt

If you are worth your salt, though you have leisure and are relieved of earning your bread, unless you work in some non-remunerative capacity and put something into the common stock of society in return for what you take out, you are as really parasites as tramps or paupers. . . . The true citizen is lofty of purpose, resolute in endeavor, ready for a hero's deeds, but never looking down on his task because it is cast in the day of small things; scornful of baseness, awake to his own duties as well as to his rights, following the higher law with reverence and in this world doing all that in his power lies, so that when death comes he may feel that mankind is in some degrees better because he lived.

It is not the critic who counts; not the man who points out how the strong man stumbled or where the doer of deeds could have done them better. The credit belongs to the man who is actually in the arena; whose face is marred by dust and sweat and blood; who strives valiantly; who errs, and comes short again and again, because there is no effort without error and shortcoming; who does actually try to do the deed; who knows the great enthusiasm, the great devotion, and spends himself in a worthy cause; who, at the best, knows in the end the triumph of high achievement, and who, at the worst, if he fails, at least fails while daring greatly. Far better is it to dare mighty things, to win glorious triumphs even though checkered by failure, than to rank with those poor spirits who neither enjoy nor suffer much because they live in the gray twilight that knows neither victory nor defeat. . . . Life's a game. Don't flinch, don't foul, and hit that line hard. Play up, play up, and play the game.

The Answer
by Grantland Rice

From *Only the Brave and Other Poems* by Grantland Rice
Copyright, 1941, by A. S. Barnes and Company, Inc.
Reprinted by permission of A. S. Barnes and Company, Inc.

When the battle breaks against you and the crowd forgets to
    cheer,
When the Anvil Chorus echoes with the essence of a jeer;
When the knockers start their panning in the knocker's nimble
    way

With a rap for all your errors and a josh upon your play—
There is one quick answer ready that will nail them on the wing;
There is one reply forthcoming that will wipe away the sting;
There is one elastic come-back that will hold them, as it should—
Make good.

No matter where you finish in the mix-up or the row,
There are those among the rabble who will pan you anyhow;
But the entry who is sticking and delivering the stuff
Can listen to the yapping as he giggles up his cuff;
The loafer has no come-back and the quitter no reply
When the Anvil Chorus echoes, as it will, against the sky;
But there's one quick answer ready that will wrap them in a
    hood—
Make good.

Success

by BERTON BRALEY from *Things As They Are*
Copyright, 1916, George H. Doran Company

If you want a thing bad enough
To go out and fight for it,
Work day and night for it,
Give up your time and your peace and your sleep for it,
If only desire of it
Makes you quite mad enough
Never to tire of it,
Makes you hold all other things tawdry and cheap for it,
If life seems all empty and useless without it
And all that you scheme and you dream is about it,
If gladly you'll sweat for it,
Fret for it,
Plan for it,
Lose all your terror of God or man for it,
If you'll simply go after that thing that you want,
With all your capacity,
Strength and sagacity,
Faith, hope and confidence, stern pertinacity,
If neither cold poverty, famished and gaunt,
Nor sickness nor pain
Of body or brain
Can turn you away from the thing that you want,
If dogged and grim you besiege and beset it,
        You'll get it!

Signs of Foul Weather

by DARWIN

From *The Every-Day Book, 1826*—An Almanac by WILLIAM HONE

Another early forecaster reveals his secrets

The hollow winds begin to blow;
The clouds look black, the glass is low;
The soot falls down, the spaniels sleep;
And spiders from their cobwebs peep.
Last night the sun went pale to bed;
The moon in halos hid her head.
The boding shepherd heaves a sigh,
For, see, a rainbow spans the sky.

The walls are damp, the ditches smell,
Closed is the pink-eyed pimpernel.
Hark! how the chairs and tables crack,
Old Betty's joints are on the rack:
Her corns with shooting pains torment her,
And to her bed untimely send her.

Loud quack the ducks, the seafowl cry,
The distant hills are looking nigh.
How restless are the snorting swine!
The busy flies disturb the kine.
Low o'er the grass the swallow wings;
The cricket too, how sharp he sings!
Puss on the hearth, with velvet paws,
Sits wiping o'er her whiskered jaws.

The smoke from chimneys right ascends,
Then spreading, back to earth it bends.
The wind unsteady veers around,
Or settling in the south is found.
Through the clear stream the fishes rise,
And nimbly catch the incautious flies.

The glowworms numerous, clear and bright,
Illum'd the dewy hill last night.
At dusk the squalid toad was seen,
Like quadruped, stalk o'er the green.
The whirling wind the dust obeys,
And in the rapid eddy plays.
The frog has changed his yellow vest,
And in a russet coat is dressed.

The sky is green, the air is still,
The mellow blackbird's voice is shrill.
The dog, so altered is his taste,
Quits mutton bones, on grass to feast.
Behold the rooks, how odd their flight;
They imitate the gliding kite,
And seem precipitate to fall,
As if they felt the piercing ball.

The tender colts on back do lie,
Nor heed the traveler passing by.
In fiery red the sun doth rise,
Then wades through clouds to mount the skies.
'Twill surely rain, we see't with sorrow,
No working in the fields tomorrow.

The Word

by John Kendrick Bangs

Today, whatever may annoy,
The word for it is Joy, just simple joy:
The joy of life;
The joy of children and of wife;
The joy of bright blue skies;
The joy of rain; the glad surprise
Of twinkling stars that shine at night;
The joy of winged things upon their flight;
The joy of noonday, and the tried,
True joyousness of eventide;
The joy of labor and of mirth;
The joy of air, and sea, and earth—
The countless joys that ever flow from Him
Whose vast beneficence doth dim
The lustrous light of day,
And lavish gifts divine upon our way.
Whate'er there be of Sorrow
I'll put off till Tomorrow,
And when Tomorrow comes, why, then
'Twill be Today, and Joy again!

* * *

Little Things

We pick up a thought
    That will last through the day;
We pick up a word
    That cheers on our way;
We pick up a friend
    Who will last through the years;
We pick up, if we will,
    More of joy than of tears;
We pick up the good
    And we pick up a smile
And 'tis these happy pickups
    That make life worth while.
                    —*Author unknown*

* * *

We depend upon others
by ALBERT EINSTEIN

Strange is our situation here upon earth. Each of us comes for a short visit, not knowing why, yet sometimes seeming to divine a purpose.

From the standpoint of daily life, however, there is one thing we do know: that man is here for the sake of other men—above all, for those upon whose smile and well-being our own happiness depends, and also for the countless unknown souls with whose fate we are connected by a bond of sympathy. Many times a day I realize how much my own outer and inner life is built upon the labors of my fellow men, both living and dead, and how earnestly I must exert myself in order to give in return as much as I have received. My peace of mind is often troubled by the depressing sense that I have borrowed too heavily from the work of other men.

Hope

Never go gloomy, man with a mind,
    Hope is a better companion than fear;
Providence, ever benignant and kind,
    Gives with a smile what you take with a tear;
        All will be right,
        Look to the light.
Morning was ever the daughter of night;
All that was black will be all that is bright,
    Cheerily, cheerily, then cheer up.

Many a foe is a friend in disguise,
    Many a trouble a blessing most true,
Helping the heart to be happy and wise,
    With love ever precious and joys ever new.
        Stand in the van,
        Strike like a man!
This is the bravest and cleverest plan;
Trusting in God while you do what you can.
    Cheerily, cheerily, then cheer up.

—Author unknown

With a Posy in His Buttonhole

by WALLACE IRWIN

I liked the way the old man stepped;
   His face was crossed with seams,
But sprightly as a child it kept
   The freshness of its dreams;
Or, like a sage, perhaps, he saw
   The way to reconcile
His gentle living to the law:
   "We pray best when we smile."
With a posy in his buttonhole—
His brow was bald, God bless his soul,
   But his step was light and strong;
His jaunty swagger seemed to click
In cadence with his walking-stick;
   With a posy in his buttonhole
      He jogged his way along.

A watcher in the parks, he sat.
   I think that he preferred
The sparrow, with its gutter-chat,
   To any singing bird,
As one, in Fate's inclemencies,
   Who did not choose to grieve
Or wear his tender tragedies
   Upon his rusty sleeve.
With a posy in his buttonhole
He puffed his pipe, and in a droll
   Young humor, passed the throng
Whom the gods hate, they first make sad!
But, being blessed in being glad,
   With a posy in his buttonhole
      He jogged along.

And some there went in broadcloth weeds,
    And long the face they drew,
And some there went in shabby tweeds—
    And his were none too new,
But when he lay, with fever parched,
    And when his light was spent
Through the gray gates of Death he marched,
    And whistled as he went.
With a posy in his buttonhole!
And where he lies, the merry soul
    I hope the blossoms say:
"Though Fate, the charlatan, be vile,
Let her not cheat you of your smile.
    Pluck a posy for your buttonhole
        And jog along your way!"

It Is Service That Counts

It isn't the cut of the clothes you wear,
  Nor the stuff out of which they are made,
Though chosen with taste and fastidious care,
  And it isn't the price that you paid;
It isn't the size of your pile in the bank,
  Nor the number of cars that you own;
It isn't a question of prestige or rank,
  Nor of sinew and muscle and bone;
It isn't the servants that come at your call,
  It isn't the things you possess,
Whether many, or little, or nothing at all—
  It's service that measures success.
It isn't a question of name or of length
  Of an ancestral pedigree,
Nor a question of mental vigor and strength,
  Nor a question of social degree;
It isn't a question of city or town,
  Nor a question of doctrine and creed;
It isn't a question of fame or renown,
  Nor a question of valorous deed;
But he who makes somebody happy, each day,
  And he who gives heed to distress,
Will find satisfaction, the richest of pay,
  For it's service that measures success.

—Author unknown

* * *

A Recipe for a Happy Life
by Margaret of Navarre

Three ounces are necessary first of patience, three of repose and peace; of conscience a pound entire is needful; of pastimes of all sorts, too, should be gathered as much as the hand can hold; of pleasant memory and of hope three good drams there must be at least, but they should rejoice the heart. Then of love's magic drops a few—but use them sparingly for they bring a flame which naught but tears can drown. Grind the whole and mix therewith of merriment an ounce to even. Yet all this may not bring happiness save in your orisons you lift your voice to Him who holds the gift of health.

Insomnia

by Thomas Bailey Aldrich

Slumber, hasten down this way,
 And, ere midnight dies,
Silence lay upon my lips,
 Darkness on my eyes.

Send me a fantastic dream;
 Fashion me afresh;
Into some celestial thing
 Change this mortal flesh.

Well I know one may not choose;
 One is helpless still
In the purple realm of Sleep:
 Use me as you will.

Let me be a frozen pine
 In dead glacier lands;
Let me pant, a leopard stretched
 On the Libyan sands.

Silver fin or scarlet wing
 Grant me, either one;
Sink me deep in emerald glooms,
 Lift me to the sun.

The Winter Robin

by Thomas Bailey Aldrich

Now is that sad time of year
When no flower or leaf is here;
When in misty Southern ways
Oriole and jay have flown,
And of all sweet birds, alone
 The robin stays.

So give thanks at Christmas-tide;
Hopes of springtime yet abide!
See, in spite of darksome days,
Wind and rain and bitter chill,
Snow, and sleet-hung branches, still
 The robin stays!

Pursuit and Possession

by THOMAS BAILEY ALDRICH

When I behold what pleasure is pursuit,
What life, what glorious eagerness it is;
Then mark how full possession falls from this,
How fairer seems the blossom than the fruit—
I am perplexed, and often stricken mute
Wondering which attained the higher bliss,
The winged insect, or the chrysalis
It thrust aside with unreluctant foot.
Spirit of verse, that still elud'st my art,
Thou uncaught rapture, thou swift-fleeting fire,
O let me follow thee with hungry heart
If beauty's full possession kill desire!
Still flit away in moonlight, rain, and dew,
Will-of-the-wisp, that I may still pursue!

Flower Garden

by THOMSON

Fair-handed Spring unbosoms every grace,
Throws out the snowdrop and the crocus first,
The daisy, primrose, violet darkly blue,
And polyanthus of unnumbered dyes,
The yellow wallflower, stained with iron brown,
The lavish stock that scents the garden round.

From the soft wing of vernal breezes shed
Anemonies, auriculas, enriched
With shining meal o'er all their velvet leaves,
And full ranunculus of glowing red.

Then comes the tulip race, where beauty plays
Her idle freaks, from family diffused
To family, as flies the father dust,
The varied colors run; and while they break
On the charmed eye, the exulting florist marks,
With secret pride, the wonders of his hand.

No gradual bloom is wanting, from the bud,
First born of Spring, to Summer's musky tribes—
Nor hyacinths of purest virgin white,
Low bent and blushing inwards—nor jonquils
Of potent fragrance—nor narcissus fair,
As o'er the fabled mountain hanging still—
Nor broad carnations, nor gay spotted pinks,
Nor showered from every bush the damask rose.

I Will

by S. E. KISER

I will start anew this morning
    with a higher, fairer creed;
I will cease to stand complaining
    of my ruthless neighbor's greed;
I will cease to sit repining
    while my duty's call is clear;
I will waste no moment whining
    and my heart shall know no fear.
I will look sometimes about me
    for the things that merit praise;
I will search for hidden beauties
    that elude the grumbler's gaze.
I will try to find contentment
    in the paths that I must tread;
I will cease to have resentment
    when another moves ahead.
I will not be swayed by envy
    when my rival's strength is shown;
I will not deny his merit,
    but I'll try to prove my own;
I will try to see the beauty
    spread before me, rain or shine;
I will cease to preach your duty
    and be more concerned with mine.

* * *

The First Julep

by BLISS CARMAN and RICHARD HOVEY

I love the lazy Southern spring,
The way she melts around a chap
And lets the great magnolias fling
Their languid petals in his lap.

I love to travel down half-way
And meet her coming up the earth,
With hurdy-gurdy men who play
And make the children dance for mirth.

But best of all I love to steer
For quiet corners not too far,
Where the first juleps reappear
With fresh green mint behind the bar.

P.S.   Perhaps you'll think it queer,
But I do not dislike a hint
To let the juleps disappear
And stick my nose into the mint.

When I Was Twenty

by Bliss Carman and Richard Hovey

It was June, and I was twenty.
All my wisdom, poor but plenty,
Never learned *Festina lente.**
Youth is gone, but whither went he?

Madeline came down the orchard
With a mischief in her eye,
Half demure and half inviting,
Melting, wayward, wistful, shy.

Four bright eyes that found life lovely,
And forgot to wonder why;
Four warm lips at one love-lesson,
Learned by heart so easily.

We gained something of that knowledge
No man ever yet put by,
But his after days of sorrow
Left him nothing but to die.

Madeline went up the orchard,
Down the hurrying world went I;
Now I know love has no morrow,
Happiness no by-and-by.

Youth is gone, but whither went he?
All my wisdom, poor but plenty,
Never learned *Festina lente.*
It was June, and I was twenty.   *To make haste slowly.*

Children's Party

by Ogden Nash, from *Verses From 1929 On*
Copyright 1935 by The Curtis Publishing Co.
Published by Little, Brown and Company

May I join you in the doghouse, Rover?
I wish to retire till the party's over.
Since three o'clock I've done my best
To entertain each tiny guest;
My conscience now I've left behind me,
And if they want me, let them find me.
I blew their bubbles, I sailed their boats,
I kept them from each other's throats.
I told them tales of magic lands,
I took them out to wash their hands.
I sorted their rubbers and tied their laces,
I wiped their noses and dried their faces.
Of similarity there's lots
'Twixt tiny tots and Hottentots.
I've earned repose to heal the ravages
Of these angelic-looking savages.
Oh, progeny playing by itself
Is a lonely fascinating elf,
But progeny in roistering batches
Would drive St. Francis from here to Natchez.

Shunned are the games a parent proposes;
They prefer to squirt each other with hoses,
Their playmates are their natural foemen
And they like to poke each other's abdomen.
Their joy needs another's woe to cushion it
Say a puddle, and somebody littler to push in it.
They observe with glee the ballistic results
Of ice cream with spoons for catapults,
And inform the assembly with tears and glares
That everyone's presents are better than theirs.
Oh, little women and little men,
Someday I hope to love you again,
But not till after the party's over,
So give me the key to the doghouse, Rover.

*

The first duty to children is to make them happy. If you
have not made them so you have wronged them. No other
good they may get can make up for that.

—Charles Buxton

*

What gift has Providence bestowed on man that is so dear
to him as his children?

—Cicero

*

Let dogs delight to bark and bite,
For God hath made them so;
Let bears and lions growl and fight,
For 'tis their nature, too.

But, children, you should never let
Such angry passions rise;
Your little hands were never made
To tear each other's eyes.

—Isaac Watts

Personal Prejudices

by Osbert Sitwell

Before the last few individuals
Are staked upon the ant-heaps
For the dear little creatures to devour,
Let me recapitulate;

I hate high deeds
Mid-high, aspiring words,
The bellow of old, blowsy buffaloes,
I love the beauty of the flowering meads
And sun-baked shepherds piping to their herds,
And waters lapping old walls, gold and rose.

I hate the clamorous voices of the crowd,
Its call for all to sacrifice for ever,
Abhor the dronings of its limpet leaders.
I love the quiet talk of those endowed
With reason—call it treason—; the endeavor
To live and love. I hate the million readers

(I love their money, but shall see it never).
I love the panther on its stealthy paws
Leaping from past to future in streaked flash.
I love to prick the bubbles, and to sever
The laws that clutter up effect with cause,
To trip the clown and then to see him crash.

I love the peasant's earth-old cunning,
The look of all things bred from a long line,
And talk up in the air, upon the ladders.
I hate the boasting first, and then the running,
The blatant brag and then regretful whine,
The bloated money-bags that burst like bladders.

I hate war's busy battles all arrayed
In dung-bright armour of old truth outworn.
I hate the clicking tongues within accustomed grooves,
I love speech to be bitter as a blade,
The unicorn with his rare ivory horn
And centaurs charging crowds with thundering hooves.

Particularly
for the Male

"The mill will never grind
with the water that has passed."

Yes, take the proverb seriously, for its lesson is serious enough! But take it cheerfully. The sound of the grinding mill may be music on a sunny day, with the diamond drops flashing as the water passes, but on a gray day, when clouds hang low, the grinding may sound like a dirge and the splashing water chill the heart. Then is the time to realize the worth of cheerfulness and resolutely defy the gray days!

Gray Days

by GRIFFITH ALEXANDER

Hang the gray days!
The deuce-to-pay days!
The feeling-blue and nothing-to-do days!
The sit-by-yourself-for-there's-nothing-new days!
When the cat that Care killed, without excuse,
With your inner self's crying, "Oh, what's the use?"
And you wonder whatever is going to become of you,
And you feel that a cipher expresses the sum of you;
And you know that you'll never,
Oh, never, be clever,
Spite of all your endeavor
Or hard work or whatever!
Oh, gee!
What a mix-up you see
When you look at the world where you happen to be!
Where strangers are hateful and friends are a bore,
And you know in your heart you will smile nevermore!
Gee, kid!
Clap on the lid!
It is all a mistake! Give your worries the skid.
There are sunny days coming,
    Succeeding the blue
And bees will be humming
    Making honey for you,
And your heart will be singing
    The merriest tune
While April is bringing
    A May and a June!

Gay days?
Playdays!
Joy-bringing paydays
And heart-lifting May days!
The sun will be shining in just a wee while,
So smile!

Necessity for Government

From *Plato's Best Thoughts*

Mankind must have laws, and conform to them, or their life would be as bad as that of the most savage beast. And the reason for this is, that no man's nature is able to know what is best for the social state of man; or knowing, always able to do what is best.

In the first place, there is a difficulty in apprehending that the true art of politics is concerned, not with private but with public good; — for public good binds together States, but private only distracts them,— nor do men always see that the gain is greater both to the individual and the State, when the State and not the individual is first considered.

In the second place, even if a person knows as a matter of science that this is the truth, but is possessed of absolute and irresponsible power, he will never be able to abide in this principle or to persist in regarding the public good as primary in the State, and the private good as secondary.

Human nature will be always drawing him into avarice and selfishness, avoiding pain and pursuing pleasure without any reason, and will bring these to the front, obscuring the juster and better; and so, working darkness in his soul, will at last fill with evils both him and the whole city. For if a man were born so divinely gifted that he could naturally apprehend the truth, he would have no need of laws to rule over him; for there is no law or order which is above knowledge, nor can mind, without impiety, be deemed the subject or slave of any man, but rather the lord of all.

A Drumlin Woodchuck

by ROBERT FROST

One thing has a shelving bank,
Another a rotting plank,
To give it cozier skies
And make up for its lack of size.

My own strategic retreat
Is where two rocks almost meet,
And still more secure and snug,
A two-door burrow I dug.

With those in mind at my back
I can sit forth exposed to attack
As one who shrewdly pretends
That he and the world are friends.

All we who prefer to live
Have a little whistle we give,
And flash, at the least alarm
We dive down under the farm.

We allow some time for guile
And don't come out for a while
Either to eat or drink.
We take occasion to think.

And if after the hunt goes past
And the double-barreled blast
(Like war and pestilence
And the loss of common sense),

If I can with confidence say
That still for another day,
Or even another year,
I will be there for you, my dear,

It will be because, though small
As measured against the All,
I have been so instinctively thorough
About my crevice and burrow.

Common sense is the knack of seeing things as they are
and doing things as they ought to be done.
                                        —*Calvin Ellis Stowe*

Not George Washington's, Not Abraham Lincoln's, But Mine

by Ogden Nash, from *Verses From 1929 On*
Copyright 1940 by The Curtis Publishing Co.
Published by Little, Brown and Company

Well, here I am thirty-eight,
Well, I certainly thought I'd have longer to wait.
You just stop in for a couple of beers,
And gosh, there go thirty-seven years.
Well, it has certainly been fun,
But I certainly thought I'd have got a lot more done.
Why if I had been really waked up and alive,
I could have been a Congressman since I was twenty-one or
    President since I was thirty-five.
I guess I know the reason my accomplishments are so measly:
I don't comprehend very easily.

It finally dawned on me that in life's race I was off to a delayed
    start
When at the age of thirty-three I had to be told that I could swim
    faster if I'd keep my fingers together instead of spreading
    them apart,
And I was convinced that precociousness was not the chief of my
    faults
When it was only last winter that I discovered that the name of
    that waltz that skaters waltz to is "The Skater's Waltz."
After thirty-seven years I find myself the kind of man that any-
    body can sell anything to,
And nobody will ever tell anything to.
Whenever people get up a party of which I am to be a member
    to see some picture which I don't want to see because I am
    uninterested in the situation that Scarlett and Mr. Chips are
    estranged over,
Why my head is what it is arranged over.
Contrariwise, I myself not only can't sell anybody anything,
I can't even ever tell anybody anything.
I have never yet had a good gossip bomb all poised and ready
    to burst
That somebody hasn't already told everybody first.
Yes, my career to date has certainly been a fiasco;
It would not have made a thrilling dramatic production for the
    late Oliver Morosco or the late David Belasco.
But in spite of the fact that my career has been a fiasco to date,
Why I am very proud and happy to be thirty-eight.

* * *

The Destroyer
by ELLA WHEELER WILCOX

With care and skill, and cunning art,
    She parried Time's malicious dart,
        And kept the years at bay,
    Till passion entered in her heart
        And aged her in a day!

* * *

Deadwood in 1876

by Judge W. L. Kuykendall, from *Frontier Days*
Copyright, 1917, by J. M. Kuykendall
Published by J. M. and H. L. Kuykendall

As men in considerable numbers and a few women began to arrive in Deadwood, it became evident that the houses along Main Street would not be sufficient, and a few of us cleared the brush and timber along Whitewood Creek, laid out lots on each side of Sherman Street, and named it South Deadwood. By this time saw-mills were in the timber, and board building soon took the place of logs. The first impression, however, upon viewing both streets was that of a log town. Nothing was done that year to grade either street. Stumps, rocks, with now and then a pine log, cumbered both, for we were simply squatters on an Indian reservation without any law for at least fifteen months.

Everybody having property was busy protecting it, building houses and roads, prospecting, mining, laying off towns, fighting Indians and burying friends and a goodly number of bad men, and had no time to grade the streets, which were left to the day when law would be in force. There was evidence that white men had many years before attemped to placer mine along Whitewood Creek above and below Deadwood, but seemingly they had never found that Deadwood Creek carried the heavy placers generally deep under the surface.

At the mouth of a gulch near the southern end of Sherman Street I stumbled over a decayed house, logs which had been cut off by a white man who was evidently a good axman. Opposite, on the hill side, numerous small dumps with prospect holes were nearly filled up by wash from above. Evidently a cabin had been built on the bank of the creek and burned by the Indians when they killed or captured and carried away for torture, the men who occupied it. Two miles below this, where the road to Custer crossed the creek, the bedrock was near the surface and two or three claims were very rich. As early as it was when I reached there, I was shown the tray of a large trunk level full of buckskin sacks full of placer gold taken out at that place. Well back in the timber, a mile or two east of this, was a very old cabin. It is reasonable to suppose that the man who had been working here had found and taken out some gold, and although the Indians greatly feared the awful thunder and lightning prevalent in this place, they had finally discovered the gold hunters and either killed or captured and disposed of them at their regular camp some distance away.

In this way they became possessed of a considerable quantity of gold dust which they used a little at a time when trading at Fort Laramie, thereby giving rise to the belief that gold was known by Indians to exist in the Black Hills. Hence they had insisted in having their treaty in 1868 stipulate that no citizens should be permitted to settle north of the North Platte River or travel in that country.

Down near Rapid Creek there was evidence of considerable prospecting by men who knew very little about the business. Probably the same party that had mined near the old cabin had started here and not finding anything, had moved up to White-wood, where they were soon discovered and wiped out by the Indians. For some time our mail was carried both ways on bull and mule trains, which occupied from four to six weeks to go and come. My place was the main improvised post office, Luke Vorhees using it for a short time after coaches commenced making trips and before a regular postmaster was appointed.

When placer gold was discovered on Deadwood Creek (so named from dead timber) during the late fall or early winter of 1875, three mining districts were organized known as the Dead-wood, Upper Whitewood and Lower Whitewood, the last being on Whitewood Creek, which was so named from the large number of white birch trees along its banks. Each had a constitution and by-laws and a recorder, as usual in such cases. Claims were three hundred feet up and down the creek and from rim to rim on each side from the creek bed.

All claimants were required to represent their claim by at least one day's work each week. Here the human hog asserted himself

again, for not satisfied with a claim in one district, quite a number of those earliest on the ground staked off and recorded a claim in each district. When large parties of men among whom there were many experienced miners arrived in the country, a near riot ensued, for they called and forced a general miners' meeting which was held in the open air about half way between Deadwood and Gayville, at which all those having claims were present with their Winchesters. The others, led by a large belligerent one-eyed miner, were also present and wanted to cut down the size of the claims.

When assured that a general killing would occur if that were attempted, the question was instantly settled, as no one seemed ready to die in that way. It was agreed that every claim must actually be worked and developed or be forfeited. The hogs either lost or sold two of their claims for small sums. One sold his claim number two, to the Wheeler Brothers. They extracted a large amount of gold, it being the richest claim on the creek. On seeing that he had reserved the wrong claim and lost a fortune, he quit the country in disgust. Thus ended the first attempted miners' rebellion in the Hills.

About this time, John Stoeber, a German from Cheyenne, who could have done well in Deadwood, came to me and said several men were going to the Big Horn Mountains and wanted him to go. I advised against it, warning him of the danger, especially where he did not know the men well enough to be sure they would all stand together in case of trouble with the Indians. Even if they would, I argued, their little party would probably never reach those mountains. And if it did, they would still be in danger after reaching there. I tried to convince him that he could do a fine business by locating and getting hold of town property. The inducements I held out had no effect as the fever was on.

They started, going by the mining camp of Bear Gulch where the miners also warned them against the foolishness of their trip, but without effect. On they went, and when fairly out of the Hills and near Red Water Creek they met a small party of Indians. A few shots were fired. They ran one way and the Indians another, over the hill and out of sight and evidently kept on running. My friend, the German, was badly wounded and could not travel, so they hurried him into the brush to die, and like the Indians, continued their flight, soon reaching the mining camp. A few miners went out immediately, found him dead, and buried him. That ended such expeditions to the Big Horn Mountains for that year.

A Rule
by JOHN WESLEY

Do all the good you can,
By all the means you can,
In all the ways you can,
In all the places you can,
At all the times you can,
To all the people you can,
As long as ever you can.

Of Studies
by FRANCIS BACON

Studies serve for pastimes, for ornaments, and for abilities. Their chief use for pastime is in privateness and retiring; for ornament is in discourse, and for ability is in judgment. For expert men can execute, but learned men are fittest to judge or censure.

To spend too much time in them is sloth; to use them too much for ornament is affectation; to make judgment wholly by their rules is the humor of a scholar.

They perfect nature, and are perfected by experience.

Crafty men contemn them, simple men admire them, wise men use them for they teach not their own use, but that there is a wisdom without them and above them, won by observation.

Read not to contradict, not to believe, but to weigh and consider.

Some books are to be tasted, others to be swallowed, and some few to be chewed and digested; that is, some books are to be read only in parts; others to be read but cursorily, and some few to be read wholly, and with diligence and attention.

Reading maketh a full man, conference a ready man, and writing an exact man. And therefore if a man write little, he had need have a great memory; if he confer little, he had need have a present wit; and if he read little, he had need have much cunning, to seem to know what he doth not.

Histories make men wise; poets, witty; mathematics, subtle; natural philosophy, deep, moral, grave; logic and rhetoric, able to contend.

Things That Are Better Than Riches

From *The Children's Bible, Selections from the Old and New Testaments*
translated and arranged by Henry A. Sherman and Charles Foster Kent
Copyright, 1922, by Charles Scribner's Sons

Better is a poor man who lives uprightly
Than one who is dishonest, though he be rich.
Better is a little with righteousness
Than great abundance with injustice.

Better is a modest spirit with the humble,
Than to divide spoil with the proud.
A good name is better than great riches,
More highly valued than silver and gold.
He who trusts in riches shall fail,
But the upright flourish like a green leaf.

Toil not that you may become rich;
Cease through your own understanding.
Should you set your eyes upon it, it is gone!
For riches fly away,
Like an eagle that flies toward heaven.
Better is little with reverence for the Lord
Than great treasure and trouble as well.

Two things I ask of thee, O God,
Deny me them not ere I die:
Put far from me deceit and lying,
Give me neither poverty nor riches;
Provide me with the food that I need,
That I may not be filled to the full and deny thee,
And say, "Who is the Lord?"
Or else be poor and steal,
And disgrace the name of my God.

The Way to Win

It takes a little courage
    And a little self-control
And some grim determination
    If you want to reach the goal;
It takes a deal of striving
    And a firm and stern-set chin,
No matter what the battle,
    If you're really out to win.

There's no easy path to glory,
   There's no rosy road to fame;
Life, however we may view it,
   Is no simple parlor game;
But its prizes call for fighting,
   For endurance and for grit,
For a rugged disposition
   And a "don't-know-when-to-quit."

You must take a blow or give one;
   You must risk and you must lose,
And expect that in the struggle
   You will suffer from a bruise;
But you mustn't wince or falter
   If a fight you once begin—
Be a man and face the battle,
   That's the only way to win!
              —Author unknown

Why Not?

From *The North American's Almanack for 1776* by SAMUEL STEARNS
An ingenious bacchanal on the earth's drinking healths

The thirsty earth soaks up the rain,
And drinks and gapes for drink again.
The plants suck in the earth, and are
With constant drinking, fresh and fair.
The sea itself, which one would think
Should have but little need of drink,
Yet drinks ten thousand rivers up,
So filled that they o'erflow the cup.
The busy sun, and one would guess
By's drunken fiery face no less,
Drinks up the sea, and when he's done,
The moon and stars drink up the sun.
They drink and dance by their own light;
They drink and revel all the night.
Nothing in nature's sober found,
But an eternal health goes round.
Fill up the bowl, then fill it high,
Fill all the glasses there; for why
Should every creature drink, but I?
Why, man of morals, tell me why?

My Five Best Dinner Companions

by Bruce Barton

Here is an interesting thought: You and I will give a dinner tonight, and our guests shall be five men we choose, out of all who have ever lived.

Whom shall we invite? . . . Napoleon? He occupies the largest space in the biographical dictionaries, and if you insist on having him I will not be stubborn about it. But I warn you at the outset that he will spoil the dinner. He was a terrible failure, you know. His greed and selfishness destroyed his talents. He might talk interestingly at the table, but he can't talk sincerely: he will almost certainly be rude, and probably be a bore.

Shall we ask Caesar or Alexander? Or Croesus, who had so much money? Or Charlemagne, who had so much power? All of them lived tumultuous lives and died by violence or in disappointment. We want no embittered old men at our supper; let's have men who succeeded, good companions, wealthy men. If you leave it to me to make up the list, I suggest these five:

First in point of years, and perhaps of interest too, I should invite that homely old fellow, Socrates. He was so wealthy in common sense! Moving about from man to man, asking his

· 84 ·

sharp questions, puncturing the toy balloons of prejudice, he probably set men to thinking wherever he went. And his power still persists. "If you kill me," he said calmly and quite impersonally to his judges, "you will not easily find another like me, who, if I may use such a ludicrous figure of speech, am a sort of gadfly, given to the State by the gods; and the State is like a great and noble steed who is tardy in his motions, owing to his very size, and requires to be stirred into life." Socrates, surely, would put life into our party.

And, if for any reason he could not come, I would give a lot to see and hear that curious fellow countryman of his, Diogenes. He was the wealthiest of all who ever lived, for he wanted absolutely nothing. "Can I do anything for you?" asked Alexander the Great, standing in the doorway of the wooden tub in which the philosopher dwelt. "Yes," replied Diogenes briskly. "Get out of my sunlight."

Dr. Samuel Johnson, because he was the world's richest talker. It was not as a talker that he hoped to be remembered. He wrote long, dull books, toiling terribly over them and expecting them to make him immortal. Nobody reads his books today, but his talk will live forever. Boswell has recorded it so perfectly that you almost see the ungainly form of the doctor and hear the rumble of his tones. He talked about everything, and always positively, with no doubt, no hesitation. When, very infrequently, the flow of words paused for a moment, Boswell was always ready with a suggestion to draw him out.

Boswell's father thought his son had wasted his life in tagging about after a penniless writer; and even Boswell himself complained a bit because the doctor kept such late hours and compelled him to absorb too much port wine. But a Mr. Dempster, about whom I know nothing except this one shrewd remark, reproved him sharply. "One had better be palsied at eighteen," he said, "than not to keep company with such a man."

Surely Sam Johnson must be in our company—a millionaire of good talk.

For myself I should like to have Samuel Pepys come. No one will claim that he was ever great, but surely in one characteristic he was richer than any man who ever lived. He possessed a boundless and insatiable curiosity. Everything interested and thrilled him—everything. A wedding or a hanging, a new tune which he could try on his flute, a meeting of Parliament, a new suit of clothes, the rearranging of his books, the odor of a well-cooked meal—these were not merely the casual occurrences of ordinary life; they were adventures, all of them.

I pity anyone who can read his diary without discovering a new capacity for enjoyment in the things of everyday life. And yet he was more than a mere recorder of petty details. There are few finer passages in literature than the concluding sentences of his diary, the writing of which he had to abandon because of the approach of blindness: "And so I betake myself to that course which is almost as much as to see myself go into the grave," he wrote, "for which, and all the discomforts that will accompany my being blind, the good God prepare me."

There was an element of the heroic in Samuel Pepys, but we are not inviting him as a hero. We want him because he would have seen so many curious and interesting things that we failed to see, and would tell about them so well.

I nominate Montaigne for our fourth guest, because he was so rich in the knowledge of himself. Emerson, on discovering Montaigne's essays, exclaimed, "It seemed to me as if I had myself written the book, in some former life, so sincerely it spoke to my thought and experience."

No franker writer ever lived than Montaigne; he was wholly free from self-deception. He observed that every man has deserved hanging five or six times, and confessed that he was no exception. "Five or six as ridiculous stories can be told of me as of any man living," he says. The sincerity of the man is inspiring; whatever happens he will not lie or equivocate; he will see and declare the truth.

Reading his words, which are so fresh and vivid after all the years, one finds new and thrilling areas within one's own consciousness. Knowing himself so well, declaring himself so completely, Montaigne discovers us to ourselves—a unique and splendid gift of service.

Finally, I should like to have Abraham Lincoln with us, because he was so rich in patience and faith. Every year new books are published about him, until the number threatens to overtake the Napoleonic total. Each emphasizes a different aspect of his character. But through them all stands the wonder of his patience, which could wait without weariness or hopelessness, and of the faith that never lost its grip, or abandoned its power to smile.

Some Comments on Slavery

by ABRAHAM LINCOLN—July 1, 1854

Equality in society alike beats inequality, whether the latter be of the British aristocratic sort or of the domestic slavery sort.

We know Southern men declare that their slaves are better off than hired laborers amongst us. How little they know whereof they speak! There is no permanent class of hired laborers amongst us. Twenty-five years ago I was a hired laborer. The hired laborer of yesterday labors on his own account today, and will hire others to labor for him tomorrow.

Advancement—improvement in condition—is the order of things in a society of equals. As labor is the common burden of our race, so the effort of some to shift their share of the burden onto the shoulders of others is the great durable curse of the race. Originally a curse for transgression upon the whole race, when, as by slavery, it is concentrated on a part only, it becomes the double-refined curse of God upon his creatures.

Free labor has the inspiration of hope; pure slavery has no hope. The power of hope upon human exertion and happiness is wonderful. The slave-master himself has a conception of it, and hence the system of tasks among slaves. The slave whom you cannot drive with the lash to break seventy-five pounds of hemp in a day, if you will task him to break a hundred, and promise him pay for all he does over, he will break you a hundred and fifty. You have substituted hope for the rod.

And yet perhaps it does not occur to you that, to the extent of your gain in the case, you have given up the slave system and adopted the free system of labor.

◆◆◆◆◆

Brilliant wits, and musing sages,
Lights who beamed through many ages,
Left to your conscious leaves their story,
And dared to trust you with their glory.

— ISAAC D'ISRAELI
From *Lines*

The Rewards of Listening
to the Advice of the Wise

From *The Children's Bible, Selections from the Old and New Testaments*
translated and arranged by Henry A. Sherman and Charles Foster Kent
Copyright, 1922, by Charles Scribner's Sons

My son, if you heed my words,
And store my commands in your mind,
Pay close attention to wisdom,
And give careful heed to reason.
If you will but seek her as silver,
And search for her as for hid treasures,
You shall then understand true religion,
And gain a knowledge of God.
For wisdom shall enter your mind,
And knowledge shall be pleasant to you,
Discretion shall watch over you,
And understanding shall guard you,
To keep you from doing wrong,
From men whose words are evil,
Who leave the paths of right
To walk in ways that are dark,
Who rejoice in doing wrong,
And take pleasure in evil deeds.

Happy the man who finds wisdom,
And he who gains understanding.
In her right hand is long life,
In her left are riches and honor.
Her ways are pleasant ways,
And all her paths are peaceful.
She gives life to those who seek her,
They are happy who hold her fast.
You shall then go on your way securely,
And your foot shall never stumble.
When you sit down, you shall not be afraid,
When you lie down, your sleep shall be sweet.

Take Each Day As It Comes

by Ralph Waldo Emerson

Write it on your heart that every day is the best day in the year. No man has learned anything rightly until he knows that every day is doomsday. Today is a king in disguise. Today always looks mean to the thoughtless, in the face of a uniform experience that all good and great and happy actions are made up precisely of these blank todays. Let us not be so deceived; let us unmask the king as he passes!

He only is rich who owns the day, and no one owns the day who allows it to be invaded with worry, fret and anxiety. Finish every day and be done with it. You have done what you could. Some blunders and absurdities no doubt crept in; forget them as soon as you can. Tomorrow is a new day; begin it well and serenely and with too high a spirit to be cumbered with your old nonsense. This day is all that is good and fair. It is too dear, with its hopes and invitations, to waste a moment on the yesterdays.

* * *

The Worries

Take yesterday's worries and sort them all out
And you'll wonder whatever you worried about.
Look back at the cares that once furrowed your brow,
I fancy you'll smile at the most of them now.
They seemed terrible then, but they really were not,
For once out of the woods all the fears are forgot.

But I'm for the Worries! I'm for the man
Who, when he's in trouble, does all that he can.
I'm for the fellow who puts up a fight
To straighten things out and make them go right.
And I say for his comfort, when matters seem bad,
Tomorrow he'll smile at the troubles he's had.

—Author unknown

* * *

The Microscopic Trout
and
the Machiavellian Fisherman

by GUY WETMORE CARRYL from *Fables for the Frivolous*

A fisher was casting his flies in a brook,
    According to laws of such sciences,
With a patented reel and a patented hook
    And a number of other appliances;
And the thirty-fifth cast, which he vowed was the last
    (It was figured as close as a decimal),
Brought suddenly out of the water a trout
    Of measurements infinitesimal.

This fish had a way that would win him a place
    In the best and most polished society,
And he looked at the fisherman full in the face
    With a visible air of anxiety:

He murmured "Alas!" from his place on the grass,
  And then, when he'd twisted and wriggled, he
Remarked in a pet that his heart was upset
  And digestion all higgledy-piggledy.

"I request," he observed, "to be instantly flung
  Once again in the pool I've been living in."
The fisherman said, "You will tire out your tongue.
  Do you see any signs of my giving in?
Put you back in the pool? Why, you fatuous fool,
  I have eaten much smaller and thinner fish.
You're not salmon or sole, but I think on the whole,
  You're a fairly respectable dinner-fish."

The fisherman's cook tried her hand on the trout
  And with various herbs she embellished him;
He was lovely to see, and there isn't a doubt
  That the fisherman's family relished him,
And, to prove that they did, both his wife and his kid
  Devoured the trout with much eagerness,
Avowing no dish could compare with that fish,
  Notwithstanding his singular meagreness.

And the moral, you'll find, is although it is kind
  To grant favors that people are wishing for,
Still a dinner you'll lack if you chance to throw back
  In the pool little trout that you're fishing for;
If their pleading you spurn you will certainly learn
  That herbs will deliciously vary 'em:
It is needless to state that a trout on a plate
  Beats several in the aquarium.

꙳

Fishing is not so much getting fishes as it is a state of mind and
a lure to the human soul into refreshment. Angling is good for
the soul of man and should be preserved as a national institution.
The increase of crime is due to a lack of those qualities of mind
and character which impregnate the soul of every fisherman—
excepting those who get no bites!

—Herbert Hoover

The blacksmith shop was where the action was in the early 1900s,
as this schoolgirl quickly discovered.

Dad Stood Tall

by Eileen M. Hasse

Courtesy of *The Milwaukee Journal*, Milwaukee, Wisconsin, U.S.A.

As the daughter of a blacksmith, I still have vivid memories of toting boxes and boxes of steel.

There were small, mysterious looking boxes. Burlap bags of irregular shapes. Sometimes a colored card which meant that there was a heavy box at the post office—one so big that my father—Theodore Pfaff—would have to get it himself.

Those were the days of solid things. Sturdy men and sturdy merchandise. Even women and children took pride in being durable.

My father's shop was a frame building covered with tarpaper that looked like brick. The sun beat down on it in summer and winter winds chilled the unheated floor unmercifully.

Unlike Longfellow's poem, there was no spreading chestnut tree over this Sauk County smithy, but the sinews in dad's arms were as strong as iron bands.

Shows Compassion

He seldom spanked me because repeat warnings simply were not necessary. I grew to love him and held him in an awe almost akin to fear.

My heart melted when his heavy brows furrowed with the burdens of a fellow man. I especially remember the compassion he showed when a farmer carried his 8-year-old daughter into the shop. She had had polio, and one leg had become shorter than the other. We were miles from a hospital with physical therapy facilities.

"If you could make a brace of sorts, that would tend to stretch the leg," the farmer said hesitantly.

Father fashioned his own design. A few days later, he proudly fastened it to the girl's leg. It was a heavy brace with springs at the side that stretched the leg with each step. The brace had to be changed, of course, as she grew. In a few years she walked without the brace, and now, a mature woman, her limp is scarcely noticeable. Dad becomes a hero all over again every time I see her.

Machine Broke Down

There were other instances when he stood ten feet tall. Like the days when an old threshing machine broke down and farmers rushed around feverishly to get it fixed. Father had to make a new part for the steam engine.

Standing by in my bibbed overalls, I felt privileged to be among them. Even though I was a girl, I was permitted to enter the world of working men because I was useful. As the eldest child in my family, I could carry tools, hold lights and get sandwiches.

Dad was the toughest man I ever saw. He was fearless— even with the wildest horses he shod. He could dress an ugly wound given him by the drill press without flinching. I've seen him drench a wound with iodine or 100 proof alcohol with no show of pain.

He was hardest, perhaps, when he returned to the shop to find that I had used his new cutting torch to make lovely butterflies for lawn ornaments from his biggest sheets of metal.

Yet his manner was almost caressing to the horses who patiently awaited his rhythmic hammering to place their shoes intact.

I grew to like the smell of horseflesh and sweaty leather. I learned to recognize the wild look when a horse got a notion to bolt, and I could quickly spot the soft look of the old four footed customers I might nuzzle.

Those were the days when some of the nicest folks I knew were horses. Those were the pleasant days when I could hang around the shop sorting bolts, cleaning cobwebs and washing the windows between errands.

The cold, blue touch of steel, the twang of hardware and the odor of fresh wood shavings mingled with horsehide became an integral part of my life.

I delighted in making rings out of horseshoe nails and kept my friends supplied with this type of "jewelry."

Air of Finality

Winters often were severe and the roads almost impassable. Farmers hauled their grist to the mill up icy hills and it was imperative that the horses be well shod. Dad had a flair for keeping the horseshoes well caulked. He took the same pride in it as a cobbler took in fitting his most distinguished customer.

One of the most interesting things in dad's shop was the old wooden tub. There was an air of finality in the way he took a newly formed piece, white hot from the forge. Using long handled tongs, he dunked it quickly into the water. Sizzling steam shot up, a tribute to a task well done. By the set of his square chin, I knew that the new piece would fit exactly where he wanted it.

Horse Trade Faded

The forge was mysterious and awesome. I always likened it to hell. The coals could be silent blue, black or white. Yet with a whiff of the bellows, it became an inferno. I always felt dad was a bit of a magician to get such malleable pieces of metal from a forge that seemed so nearly dead.

Dad's rhythmic "shoe-a-horse, shoe-a-horse, rat-a-tat-tat" filled the shop with music.

"Do you think I am simply hammering on the anvil?" he asked me one day. "No, I'm beating out a tune. Every life needs music and if you learn to sing with your work you will always find sunshine. A singing worker never withers."

It was true that the bounce of his hammer was music. Sometimes I recognized the tunes he played on his trumpet with the village band. Other times, I could guess by his smile that he was beating out an old-time song that gave him pleasure.

He taught me many other values, too—values that fit as deeply as the caulks on his horseshoes.

The shop lost a little warmth and humanity when horses began to disappear. Little by little the horse corner in the shop filled up with machinery. Then an extra room was added to accommodate tractors. Gradually the old shop began to smell of gas and oil—and the odor of sweaty flesh and old leather disappeared.

I was glad I was getting too old to hang around the shop anyway. I didn't take the time to examine the acetylene welder and then the electric welder with its blinding light.

Eventually, women and stainless steel found their way to the shop. Electrical gadgets, fancy chairs and goods took over. Boxes of steel still arrive by a special parcel delivery service, but gone are the men of steel—the hard fisted, tobacco chewing men whose spicy banter provided such fascinating listening.

Today, after fifty years as a smith, dad gets around with a cane and still visits the old shop most every day. From an armchair near the door, he watches my brother, Robert, fix most everything but broken hearts.

Guided Aggression Should Be the Aim of Youth
by RAY LYMAN WILBUR

Fortunately, all do not achieve maturity at the same time! Some do not accomplish that until they get in their sixties, but many achieve senility very early. It is a constant struggle between these groups: those dead, half dead, and those still moving. It is so easy to have all kinds of motions and emotions in life and have those apparently make up the whole.

Direction is what we want, direction of these impulses. The people who give it must have a deep sympathy for youth, whether they be parents or teachers. They must realize that times change and people must change with them but that firm essentials of life, the fundamentals, stay on just about the same. It is difficult for older people to avoid senile thinking.

It is difficult for us not to put too high a credit on docility in youth. The thing that many teachers give the greatest rewards for is docility. Do not put too much faith in that. Guided aggression, guided advance, youth under power and impulse and going ahead in the right direction with the spiritual element in it—that is the thing for which we wish to stand.

Ready for Promotion

by Edgar A. Guest, from *The Friendly Way*
Copyright 1931 by The Reilly & Lee Company

There's going to be a vacancy above you later on;
Some day you'll find the foreman or the superintendent gone,
And are you growing big enough, when this shall be the case,
To quit the post you're holding now and step into his place?

You do the work you have to do with ease from day to day,
But are you getting ready to deserve the larger pay?
If there should come a vacancy with bigger tasks to do,
Could you step in and fill the place if it were offered you?

Tomorrow's not so far away, nor is the goal you seek;
Today you should be training for the work you'll do next week.
The bigger job is just ahead, each day new changes brings—
Suppose that post were vacant now, could you take charge of things?

It's not enough to know enough to hold your place today;
It's not enough to do enough to earn your weekly pay;
Some day there'll be a vacancy with greater tasks to do—
Will you be ready for the place when it shall fall to you?

Forever and a Day

by Thomas Bailey Aldrich

I little know or care
If the blackbird on the bough
Is filling all the air
With his soft crescendo now;
  For she is gone away,
  And when she went she took
  The springtime in her look,
  The peachblow on her cheek,
  The laughter from the brook,
  The blue from out the May—
  And what she calls a week
  Is forever and a day!

It's little that I mind
How the blossoms, pink or white,

At every touch of wind
Fall a-trembling with delight;
    For in the leafy lane,
    Beneath the garden-boughs,
    And through the silent house
    One thing alone I seek.
    Until she comes again
    The May is not the May,
    And what she calls a week
    Is forever and a day!

The Pessimist

by BEN KING

Nothing to do but work,
    Nothing to eat but food,
Nothing to wear but clothes
    To keep one from going nude.

Nothing to breathe but air
    Quick as a flash 'tis gone;
Nowhere to fall but off,
    Nowhere to stand but on.

Nothing to comb but hair,
    Nowhere to sleep but in bed,
Nothing to weep but tears,
    Nothing to bury but dead.

Nothing to sing but songs,
    Ah, well, alas! alack!
Nowhere to go but out,
    Nowhere to come but back.

Nothing to see but sights,
    Nothing to quench but thirst,
Nothing to have but what we've got;
    Thus thro' life we are cursed.

Nothing to strike but a gait;
    Everything moves that goes.
Nothing at all but common sense
    Can ever withstand these woes.

The Evils of Rum

From *The North American's Almanack for 1776* by SAMUEL STEARNS

Sir Richard Rum's Advice to the Soldiers and Others

Gentlemen,

The many good deeds that I, the great, celebrated Sir Richard, have done among you cannot fail of exciting in you the highest veneration for me in these difficult times. The thoughts of this veneration have much encouraged me to give you the following important and weighty directions, for I know that the voice of every gentleman that is in as good credit and has as much power and influence as myself hardly ever fails of being heard and obeyed.

Now I imagine that you have also a very good veneration for my tnree kinsmen—I mean my Uncle Cider, Brother Brandy, and Cousin Wine—for these three gentlemen have done much good in the camp as well as myself. It has been observed that my Brother and Cousin, together with myself when we are used with moderation, do make the three greatest cordials that this world affords, for we elevate the minds of them that are dejected, cheer and refresh the spirits of them that are in a languishing condition, we strengthen the viscera and promote digestion, we invigorate the blood, and, in a word, assist nature in performing all her functions. My Uncle Cider, though he is a more sour and crabbed gentleman than myself, will, if he is prudently used, assist in performing the above wonders, but when any of us are used to excess and without moderation, we heat the blood, disturb the secretions, corrupt the fluids, cause drunkenness, create fevers and many chronic diseases, such as palsies, dropsies, lethargies, apoplexies, and so forth.

I, the great Sir Richard Rum, who am a gentleman of a noble birth and extraction and who am invested with such great power and authority that I govern the mind and command the purses of many Americans, am now come to caution every soldier and every other person against the using of me too freely, for I knock up the heels of them that abuse me and throw them flat on their backs, by which they often get their joints dislocated and their bones broken. It makes me feel very melancholy when I consider how often men lose their lives by drunkenness, and how much this vice increases and abounds where the company of me, the great Sir Richard, can be had; for though I am a creature that is innocent, harmless, and blameless in mine own nature, and one that meddles with nobody's business but my own, yet we see how often I am forced into bad company and kept there till I am abused to a very high degree. I will now communicate to you a certain cure for a person that is drunk.

First—Let the drunkard's head be raised, and to his nose apply a sponge dipped in vinegar.

Secondly—Give him warm water mixed with vinegar to drink.

Thirdly—Let him be blooded.

Fourthly—Give him a gentle emetic.

Fifthly—Set his feet in cold water.

Sixthly and lastly—Inject a laxative enema.

I have been much grieved in these troublesome times at the melancholy situation of the British nation, which is now divided against itself. It troubles me much to think that I, the great Sir Richard, am forced against my conscience to fight on both sides. I heartily wish that the difficulties in the nation might subside. I must wind off at this time by giving the following advice to every soldier and every American, namely—rob not the King, nor thyself. Farewell. I am your kind friend and humble servant,

Richard Rum

All Is Well That Ends Well

From *The North American's Almanack for 1776* by SAMUEL STEARNS

If I this proverb unto you explain,
I hope my pen won't be employed in vain;
And whilst I do upon this matter act,
I will declare to you that which is fact:
That though the end doth trouble often bring,
Yet 'tis the end that doth crown everything.
Whilst I proceed, I will to you tell this,
That everything should not be judged amiss,
That doth appear so in these present times,
As they may happen for our wicked crimes;
A fit of sickness may us much befriend
If we thereby our vicious lives do mend,
By bad misfortunes we may quickened be
To diligence and good industry.
Though for the present no affliction seems
Joyous but grievous, yet it is a means
If well improved, to lead us in our way,
To the bright regions of immortal day;
A good reward is always the event,
Of everyone whose life is rightly spent;
If we in judging would mistakes prevent,
Let us look at the issue and event
Of things, or else most surely we can't tell,
Whether the end of things is bad or well.

The Humility of Franklin

*Letter from Benjamin Franklin to an engraver in Paris
respecting a print commemorative of American independence*

Passy, France, June 24, 1778

Sir: On reading again the prospectus and explanation of your intended print, I find the whole merit of giving freedom to America continues to be ascribed to me, which, as I told you in our first conversation, I could by no means approve of, as it would be unjust to the number of wise and brave men who, by their arms and counsels, have shared in the enterprise and contributed to its success (as far as it has yet succeeded) at the hazard of their lives and fortunes.

My proposition to you was, and continues to be, that, instead of naming me in particular in the explanation of the print, it should be said, "The Congress, represented by a Senator in Roman dress, etc." As it stands, I cannot consent to accept the honor you propose to do me by dedicating the print to me, which I understand, is in this country considered as an approbation; and in my own country it would hurt my character and usefulness if I were to give the least countenance to such a pretension by recommending or proposing the sale of a print so explained.

Upon these considerations, I must request that, if you are determined to proceed in the engraving, you would, in a new prospectus, change the explanation as above proposed, and dedicate the print not to me, but to the Congress.

Wishing

by JOHN G. SAXE

Of all amusements for the mind,
From logic down to fishing,
There isn't one that you can find
So very cheap as "wishing."
A very choice diversion too,
If we but rightly use it,
And not, as we are apt to do,
Pervert it, and abuse it.

I wish — a common wish indeed —
   My purse were somewhat fatter,
That I might cheer the child of need,
   And not my pride to flatter;
That I might make Oppression reel,
   As only gold can make it,
And break the Tyrant's rod of steel,
   As only gold can break it.

I wish — that Sympathy and Love,
   And every human passion,
That has its origin above,
   Would come and keep in fashion;
That Scorn, and Jealousy, and Hate,
   And every base emotion,
Were buried fifty fathom deep
   Beneath the waves of Ocean!

I wish — that friends were always true,
   And motives always pure;
I wish the good were not so few,
   I wish the bad were fewer;
I wish that parsons ne'er forgot
   To heed their pious teaching;
I wish that practicing were not
   So different from preaching!

I wish — that modest worth might be
   Appraised with truth and candor;
I wish that innocence were free
   From treachery and slander;
I wish that men their vows would mind;
   That women ne'er were rovers;
I wish that wives were always kind,
   And husbands always lovers!

I wish — in fine — that Joy and Mirth,
   And every good Ideal,
May come erelong, throughout the earth,
   To be the glorious Real;
Till God shall every creature bless
   With his supremest blessing,
And Hope be lost in Happiness,
   And Wishing in Possessing!

Before the Days of Satellite Weather-Watchers the Farmers Had Their Own Signs to Forecast Weather

From *The Every-Day Book, 1826*—An Almanac by WILLIAM HONE

To be able to ascertain the future changes of the weather is of infinite use to the farmer and gardener. Animals are evidently sooner sensible of the ensuing change of the atmosphere than we are, and from their divers appearances and apparent sensations we may in many instances determine what changes are likely to take place. The following may be set down as general rules, and upon minute observation we shall find them correct.

When the raven is observed early in the morning at a great height in the air, soaring round and round and uttering a hoarse croaking sound, we may be sure the day will be fine, and may conclude the weather is about to clear and become fair.

The loud and clamorous quacking of ducks, geese, and other water-fowl is a sign of rain.

Before rain swine appear very uneasy and rub in the dust, as do cocks and hens.

Before storms cows and also sheep assemble at one corner of the field and are observed to turn all their heads toward the quarter from whence the wind doth not blow.

The appearance of sea gulls, petrels, or other sea fowl in the inlands indicates stormy weather.

In fine weather the bat is observed to continue flying about very late of an evening.

In autumn before rain some flies bite, and others become very troublesome, and gnats are more apt to sting.

When flocks of wild geese are observed flying in a westward or southern direction in autumn, it indicates a hard winter.

The floating of gossamer and its alighting on the rigging of ships foretells fine weather.

The clamorous croaking of frogs indicates rainy weather.

The appearance of beetles flying about of an evening in summer indicates that the next day will be fair.

Before rain dogs are apt to grow very sleepy and dull, and to lie all day before the fire.

Before rain moles throw up the earth more than usual.

The appearance of rare foreign birds in this country, such as rollers, hoopoos, and so forth, indicates hard weather.

When spiders are seen crawling on the walls more than usual, rain will probably ensue.

The much barking of dogs in the night frequently indicates a change in the weather.

When the trees and hedges are very full of berries, it indicates a hard winter.

The abundance of woodseare and honeydew on herbs indicates fair weather, as does floating gossamer.

It is said in Wiltshire that the dunpickles or moor buzzards alight in great numbers on the downs before rain.

Before storms the missel thrush is observed to sing particularly loud, and to continue so till the commencement of the rain, from which circumstance it is in some places called the storm cock.

It is a sign of rain when pigeons return slowly to the dovehouses.

When bees do not go out as usual, but keep in or about their hives, rain may be expected.

Before wind swine run squeaking about as though they were mad, which has given rise to the notion that pigs can see the wind.

Before rain the pintados called comebacks squall more than usual, as do peacocks.

The early appearance of woodcocks, snipes, swinepipes, fieldfares, and so forth, are prognostications of severe winters.

When the dew lies plenteously upon the grass in the evening, the next day will probably be fine; when there is little or no dew, probably wet.

Dr. Forster observes, on the authority of Virgil, that "the blowing about of feathers or any light substances on the water is also a sign of rain."

A Nook and a Book

by WILLIAM FREELAND, from *A Birth Song and Other Poems*

Give me a nook and a book,
    And let the proud world spin round;
Let it scramble by hook or by crook
    For wealth or a name with a sound.
You are welcome to amble your ways,
    Aspirers to place or to glory;
May big bells jangle your praise,
    And golden pens blazon your story!
For me, let me dwell in my nook,
Here by the curve of this brook,
That croons to the tune of my book,
Whose melody wafts me forever
On the waves of an unseen river.

Give me a book and a nook
    Far away from the glitter and strife;
Give me a staff and a crook,
    The calm and the sweetness of life;
Let me pause — let me brood as I list,
    On the marvels of heaven's own spinning —
Sunlight and moonlight and mist,
    Glorious without slaying or sinning.
Vain world, let me reign in my nook,
King of this kingdom, my book,
A region by fashion forsook;
Pass on, ye lean gamblers for glory,
Nor mar the sweet tune of my story!

The Un-Americans

by Russell Baker

"Sit down, son. I'd like to talk to you."

"Not about the hair again!"

"Not about the hair."

"Not about closing down that rotten university you sent me to!"

"Not about that. Not even about provoking the police."

"Well, what then?"

"About the House Un-American Activities Committee."

"Never heard of it."

"Of course not. It's been dormant for years, but it's stirring again. It's summoned some of the New Left to Washington next week, and if we have a real political repression next year it might get you too."

"What for?"

"For whatever you did last year that Congress decides next year is un-American."

"Speak English. What have I done that's un-American?"

"Anything that some member of the committee might not like one of these days."

"They don't like what I'm doing right now. That's why I'm doing it, man."

"I know. And that's why you should always ask yourself, before you do anything, not only is it American right now? But also, will it be American five years from now?"

"Say it in four-letter words, Dad. I don't understand."

*   *   *

"Look, you're before the committee. It's 1970. The whole country is angry at the idea that in 1968 people wore long hair. In 1970, long hair is un-American. You're put in the witness chair before 200 reporters, and the congressman says, did you, on or about Sept. 25, 1968, wear hair that was shoulder length? If you say yes, there will be headlines screaming "Admits to Hair." If you say no, they'll charge you with perjury. Either way you're ruined."

"You're putting me on."

"That's what it's like in a political repression when the committees start chopping heads, son."

"Man, that's crazy. Like pool with a twisted cue. Look, have they got a list of American activities that it's all right to participate in? I mean, activities like washing the car, keeping your shoes shined, that kind of thing?"

"Don't be frivolous, boy. You know very well it's American to wash your car and keep your shoes shined. They're interested in making sure that your political activities are American."

"Well, tell me some political activities that are un-American."

"That hasn't been decided yet. It won't be decided until the new Congress meets. Then we'll know what activities the voters are angry about and want to see somebody ruined for participating in. Those will be un-American activities and if you're unlucky enough to have participated in them at some time you'll probably be ruined."

* * *

"You old fellows really bug me. I mean, look, here I am, the soul of uplift, a puritan in rags. I reduce everything to an issue of morality. I go around sermonizing the country about right and wrong. I'm so gone on love that I hate anybody who doesn't do it. I'm against corruption, evil and hypocrisy and, like a good American, I never give anybody a chance to forget it. What could possibly be more American than that?"

"You're young, son. You don't understand. When things go wrong, people get angry and they want the committees to find somebody who can be ruined. It's not a question of how American you may be, but whether the people you are opposing win the next election."

"Hah! That's typical of the injustice we get from our corrupt system. But just wait. One of these days, I'll be on the winning side."

"I hope so, son. Then you can abolish the committee."

"Abolish it! You're putting me on. When that time comes I'll need it to go after the real un-Americans."

O Rattler of Matchless Fame
by BEN BURN from *Boxiana*

O, Rattler, chief of all the clan
Of fancy dogs—revered by man,
   Thou well deserv'st my lay;
Thou pride and boast of fancy's grace,
And hero of the canine race,
   Surpasses all our praise.

Thy gentle nature—always mild—
Indulgent to a harmless child,
  Unless spurned on to strife—
Like to a lamb you meet the fray,
And lion-hearted, gain the day
  Of victory or life.

What language can thy merits tell!
In twenty battles bare the bell,
  Though few years you have seen;
The knowing ones now know your name,
The Prince of Dogs, of matchless fame—
  Your equal has not been.

But now your master, for your good,
Will not again stir up your blood,
  But keep you in soft rest,
T'indulge the remainder of your days
In peaceful mood, your playful ways,
  And still by him caressed.

Achieving Good Health and Good Condition in the 19th Century

From *Boxiana; or, Sketches of Modern Pugilism during the years 1821, 1822, 1823*

It has been made a question, whether training produces a *lasting,* or only a *temporary* effect on the constitution. It is undeniable that if a man be brought to a better condition—if corpulency and the impurities of his body disappear, and if his wind and strength be improved by any process whatever—his good state of health will continue, until some derangement of his frame shall take place from accidental or natural causes.

If he will relapse into intemperance, or neglect the means of preserving his health, either by omitting to take the necessary exercise or by indulging in debilitating propensities, he must expect such encroachments to be made on his constitution as must soon unhinge his system. But if he will observe a different plan, the beneficial effects of the training process will remain until the gradual decay of his natural functions shall, in mature old age, intimate the approach of his dissolution.

The ancients entertained this opinion. "They were," says Dr. Buchan, "by no means unacquainted with, or inattentive to, these instruments of medicine, although modern practitioners appear to have no idea of removing disease, or restoring health, except by pouring drugs into the stomach."

Herodicus is said to have been the first who applied the exercises and regimen of the gymnasium to the removal of disease, or the maintenance of health.

Among the Romans, Asclepiades carried this so far that he is said by Celsus almost to have banished the use of internal remedies from his practice. He was the inventor of pensile beds, which were used to induce sleep, and of various other modes of exercise and gestation, and rose to great eminence as a physician in Rome. In his own person he afforded an excellent example of the wisdom of his rules, and the propriety of his regimen.

Pliny tells us that, in early life, he made a public profession that he would agree to forfeit all pretensions to the name of a physician, should he ever suffer from sickness, or die but of old age; and, what is more extraordinary, he fulfilled his promise, for he lived upwards of a century, and at last was killed by a fall downstairs.

On the Blue Water

by Ernest Hemingway

Certainly there is no hunting like the hunting of man and those who have hunted armed men long enough and liked it, never really care for anything else thereafter. You will meet them doing various things with resolve, but their interest rarely holds because after the other thing ordinary life is as flat as the taste of wine when the taste buds have been burned off your tongue. Wine, when your tongue has been burned clean with lye and water, feels like puddle water in your mouth, while mustard feels like axle-grease, and you can smell crisp, fried bacon, but when you taste it, there is only a feeling of crinkly lard.

You can learn about this matter of the tongue by coming into the kitchen of a villa on the Riviera late at night and taking a drink from what should be a bottle of Evian water and which turns out to be *Eau de Javel*, a concentrated lye product used for cleaning sinks. The taste buds on your tongue, if burned off by *Eau de Javel*, will begin to function again after about a week. At what rate other things regenerate one does not know, since you lose track of friends and the things one could learn in a week were mostly learned a long time ago.

The other night I was talking with a good friend to whom all hunting is dull except elephant hunting. To him there is no sport in anything unless there is great danger and, if the danger is not enough, he will increase it for his own satisfaction. A hunting companion of his had told me how this friend was not satisfied with the risks of ordinary elephant hunting but would, if possible, have the elephants driven, or turned, so he could take them head-on, so it was a choice of killing them with the difficult frontal shot as they came, trumpeting, with their ears spread, or having them run over him. This is to elephant hunting what the German cult of suicide climbing is to ordinary mountaineering, and I suppose it is, in a way, an attempt to approximate the old hunting of the armed man who is hunting you.

This friend was speaking of elephant hunting and urging me to hunt elephant, as he said that once you took it up no other hunting would mean anything to you. I was arguing that I enjoyed all hunting and shooting, any sort I could get, and had no desire to wipe this capacity for enjoyment out with the *Eau de Javel* of the old elephant coming straight at you with his trunk up and his ears spread.

"Of course you like that big fishing too," he said rather sadly. "Frankly, I can't see where the excitement is in that."

"You'd think it was marvelous if the fish shot at you with Tommy guns or jumped back and forth through the cockpit with swords on the ends of their noses."

"Don't be silly," he said. "But frankly I don't see where the thrill is."

"Look at so and so," I said. "He's an elephant hunter and this last year he's gone fishing for big fish and he's goofy about it. He must get a kick out of it or he wouldn't do it."

"Yes," my friend said. "There must be something about it but I can't see it. Tell me where you get a thrill out of it."

"I'll try to write it in a piece sometime," I told him.

"I wish you would," he said. "Because you people are sensible on other subjects. Moderately sensible I mean."

"I'll write it."

In the first place, the Gulf Stream and the other great ocean currents are the last wild country there is left. Once you are out of sight of land and of the other boats you are more alone than you can ever be hunting and the sea is the same as it has been since before men ever went on it in boats. In a season fishing you will see it oily flat as the becalmed galleons saw it while they drifted to the westward; white-capped with a fresh breeze as they saw it running with the trades; and in high, rolling blue hills the tops blowing off them like snow as they were punished by it, so that sometimes you will see three great hills of water with your fish jumping from the top of the farthest one and if you tried to make a turn to go with him without picking your chance, one of those breaking crests would roar down in on you with a thousand tons of water and you would hunt no more elephants, Richard, my lad.

There is no danger from the fish, but anyone who goes on the sea the year around in a small power boat does not seek danger. You may be absolutely sure that in a year you will have it without seeking, so you try always to avoid it all you can.

Because the Gulf Stream is an unexploited country, only the very fringe of it ever being fished, and then only a dozen places in thousands of miles of current, no one knows what fish live in it, or how great size they reach or what age, or even what kinds of fish and animals live in it at different depths. When you are drifting, out of sight of land, fishing four lines, sixty, eighty, one hundred and one hundred fifty fathoms down, in water that is seven hundred fathoms deep you never know what may take the small tuna that you use for bait, and every time the line starts to run off the reel, slowly first, then with a scream of the click as the rod bends and you feel it double and the huge weight of the friction of the line rushing through that depth of water while you pump and reel, pump and reel, pump and reel, trying to get the belly out of the line before the fish jumps, there is always a thrill that needs no danger to make it real. It may be a marlin that will jump high and clear off to your right and then go off in a series of leaps, throwing a splash like a speedboat in a sea as you shout for the boat to turn with him watching the line melting off the reel before the boat can get around. Or it may be a broadbill that will show wagging his great broadsword. Or it may be some fish that you will never see at all that will head straight out to the northwest like a submerged submarine and never show and at the end of five hours the angler has a straightened-out hook. There is always a feeling of excitement when a fish takes hold when you are drifting deep.

In hunting you know what you are after and the top you can get is an elephant. But who can say what you will hook sometime when drifting in a hundred and fifty fathoms in the Gulf Stream? There are probably marlin and swordfish to which the fish we have seen caught are pygmies; and every time a fish takes the bait drifting you have a feeling perhaps you are hooked to one of these.

Carlos, our Cuban mate, who is fifty-three years old and has been fishing for marlin since he went in the bow of a skiff with his father when he was seven, was fishing drifting deep one time when he hooked a white marlin. The fish jumped twice and then sounded and when he sounded suddenly Carlos felt a great weight and he could not hold the line which went out and down and down irresistibly until the fish had taken out over a hundred and fifty fathoms. Carlos says it felt as heavy and solid as though he were hooked to the bottom of the sea. Then suddenly the strain was loosened but he could feel the weight of his original fish and pulled it up stone dead. Some toothless fish like a swordfish or marlin had closed his jaws across the middle of the eighty pound white marlin and squeezed it and held it so that every bit of the insides of the fish had been crushed out while the huge fish moved off with the eighty-pound fish in its mouth. Finally it let go. What size of a fish would that be? I thought it might be a giant squid but Carlos said there were no sucker marks on the fish and that it showed plainly the shape of the marlin's mouth where he had crushed it.

Another time an old man fishing alone in a skiff out of Cabañas hooked a great marlin that, on the heavy sashcord handline, pulled the skiff far out to sea. Two days later the old man was picked up by fishermen sixty miles to the eastward, the head and forward part of the marlin lashed alongside. What was left of the fish, less than half, weighed eight hundred pounds. The old man had stayed with him a day, a night, a day and another night while the fish swam deep and pulled the boat. When he had come up the old man had pulled the boat up on him and harpooned him. Lashed alongside the sharks had hit him and the old man had fought them out alone in the Gulf Stream in a skiff, clubbing them, stabbing at them, lunging at them with an oar until he was exhausted and the sharks had eaten all that they could hold. He was crying in the boat when the fishermen picked him up, half crazy from his loss, and the sharks were still circling the boat.

But what is the excitement in catching them from a launch? It comes from the fact that they are strange and wild things of unbelievable speed and power and a beauty, in the water and leaping, that is indescribable, which you would never see if you did not fish for them, and to which you are suddenly harnessed so that you feel their speed, their force and their savage power as intimately as if you were riding a bucking horse. For half an hour, an hour, or five hours, you are fastened to the fish as much as he is fastened to you and you tame him and break him the way a wild horse is broken and finally lead him to the boat. For pride and because the fish is worth plenty of money in the Havana market, you gaff him at the boat and bring him on board, but the having him in the boat isn't the excitement; it is while you are fighting him that is the fun.

If the fish is hooked in the bony part of the mouth I am sure the hook hurts him no more than the harness hurts the angler. A large fish when he is hooked often does not feel the hook at all and will swim toward the boat, unconcerned, to take another bait. At other times he will swim away deep, completely unconscious of the hook, and it is when he feels

himself held and pressure exerted to turn him, that he knows
something is wrong and starts to make his fight. Unless he is
hooked where it hurts he makes his fight not against the pain
of the hook, but against being captured and if, when he is out
of sight, you figure what he is doing, in what direction he is
pulling when deep down, and why, you can convince him and
bring him to the boat by the same system you break a wild
horse. It is not necessary to kill him, or even completely exhaust
him to bring him to the boat.

To kill a fish that fights deep you pull against the direction
he wants to go until he is worn out and dies. It takes hours
and when the fish dies the sharks are liable to get him before
the angler can raise him to the top. To catch such a fish quickly
you figure by trying to hold him absolutely, which direction
he is working (a sounding fish is going in the direction the
line slants in the water when you have put enough pressure
on the drag so the line would break if you held it any tighter);
then get ahead of him on that direction and he can be brought
to the boat without killing him. You do not tow him or pull
him with the motor boat; you use the engine to shift your
position just as you would walk up or down stream with a
salmon. A fish is caught most surely from a small boat such
as a dory since the angler can shut down on his drag and simply
let the fish pull the boat. Towing the boat will kill him in time.
But the most satisfaction is to dominate and convince the fish
and bring him intact in everything but spirit to the boat as
rapidly as possible.

"Very instructive," says the friend. "But where does the
thrill come in?"

The thrill comes when you are standing at the wheel drinking a cold bottle of beer and watching the outriggers jump the
baits so they look like small live tuna leaping along and then
behind one you see a long dark shadow wing up and then a
big spear thrust out followed by an eye and head and dorsal
fin and the tuna jumps with the wave and he's missed it.

"Marlin," Carlos yells from the top of the house and stamps
his feet up and down, the signal that a fish is raised. He swarms
down to the wheel and you go back to where the rod rests in
its socket and there comes the shadow again, fast as the shadow
of a plane moving over the water, and the spear, head, fin and
shoulders smash out of water and you hear the click the close-
pin makes as the line pulls out and the long bight of line
whishes through the water as the fish turns and as you hold

the rod, you feel it double and the butt kicks you in the belly as you come back hard and feel his weight, as you strike him again and again, and again.

Then the heavy rod arc-ing out toward the fish, and the reel in a band-saw zinging scream, the marlin leaps clear and long, silver in the sun long, round as a hogshead and banded with lavender stripes and, when he goes into the water, it throws a column of spray like a shell lighting.

Then he comes out again, and the spray roars, and again, then the line feels slack and out he bursts headed across and in, then jumps wildly twice more seeming to hang high and stiff in the air before falling to throw the column of water and you can see the hook in the corner of his jaw.

Then in a series of jumps like a greyhound he heads to the northwest and standing up, you follow him in the boat, the line taut as a banjo string and little drops coming from it until you finally get the belly of it clear of that friction against the water and have a straight pull out toward the fish.

And all the time Carlos is shouting, "Oh, God the bread of my children! Oh look at the bread of my children! Joseph and Mary look at the bread of my children jump! There it goes the bread of my children! He'll never stop the bread the bread the bread of my children!"

This striped marlin jumped, in a straight line to the north-west, fifty-three times, and every time he went out it was a sight to make your heart stand still. Then he sounded and I said to Carlos, "Get me the harness. Now I've got to pull him up the bread of your children."

"I couldn't stand to see it," he says. "Like a filled pocket-book jumping. He can't go down deep now. He's caught too much air jumping."

"Like a race horse over obstacles," Julio says. "Is the harness all right? Do you want water?"

"No." Then kidding Carlos, "What's this about the bread of your children?"

"He always says that," says Julio. "You should hear him curse me when we would lose one in the skiff."

"What will the bread of your children weigh?" I ask with mouth dry, the harness taut across shoulders, the rod a flexible prolongation of the sinew pulling ache of arms, the sweat salty in my eyes.

"Four hundred and fifty," says Carlos.

"Never," says Julio.

"Thou and thy never," says Carlos. "The fish of another always weighs nothing to thee."

"Three seventy-five," Julio raises his estimate. "Not a pound more."

Carlos says something unprintable and Julio comes up to four hundred.

The fish is nearly whipped now and the dead ache is out of raising him, and then, while lifting, I feel something slip. It holds for an instant and then the line is slack.

"He's gone," I say and unbuckle the harness.

"The bread of your children," Julio says to Carlos.

"Yes," Carlos says. "Yes. Joke and no joke yes. *El pan de mis hijos*. Three hundred and fifty pounds at ten cents a pound.

How many days does a man work for that in the winter? How cold is it at three o'clock in the morning on all those days? And the fog and the rain in a norther. Every time he jumps the hook cutting the hole a little bigger in his jaw. Ay how he could jump. How he could jump!"

"The bread of your children," says Julio.

"Don't talk about that any more," said Carlos.

No it is not elephant hunting. But we get a kick out of it. When you have a family and children, your family, or my family, or the family of Carlos, you do not have to look for danger. There is always plenty of danger when you have a family.

And after a while the danger of others is the only danger and there is no end to it nor any pleasure in it nor does it help to think about it.

But there is great pleasure in being on the sea, in the unknown wild suddenness of a great fish; in his life and death which he lives for you in an hour while your strength is harnessed to his; and there is satisfaction in conquering this thing which rules the sea it lives in.

Then in the morning of the day after you have caught a good fish, when the man who carried him to the market in a handcart brings the long roll of heavy silver dollars wrapped in a newspaper on board it is very satisfactory money. It really feels like money.

"There's the bread of your children," you say to Carlos.

"In the time of the dance of the millions," he says, "a fish like that was worth two hundred dollars. Now it is thirty. On the other hand a fisherman never starves. The sea is very rich."

"And the fisherman always poor."

"No. Look at you. You are rich."

"Like hell," you say. "And the longer I fish the poorer I'll be. I'll end up fishing with you for the market in a dinghy."

"That I never believe," says Carlos devoutly. "But look. That fishing in a dinghy is very interesting. You would like it."

"I'll look forward to it," you say.

"What we need for prosperity is a war," Carlos says. "In the time of the war with Spain and in the last war the fishermen were actually rich."

"All right," you say. "If we have a war you get the dinghy ready."

Stubble and Slough in Dakota

From *Pony Tracks*, written and illustrated by FREDERIC REMINGTON

Now I am conscious that all my life I have seen men who owned shotguns and setter-dogs, and that these persons were wont at intervals to disappear from their usual haunts with this paraphernalia. Without thinking, I felt that they went to slay little birds, and for them I entertained a good-natured contempt. It came about in this wise that I acquired familiarity with "mark," and "hie-on," and "No. 6 vis No. 4's": by telegram I was invited to make one of a party in Chicago, bound West on a hunting expedition. It being one of my periods of unrest, I promptly packed up my Winchester, boots, saddle, and blankets, wired "All right—next train," and crawled into the "Limited" at Forty-second Street.

"West" is to me a generic term for that country in the United States which lies beyond the high plains, and this will account for my surprise when I walked into the private car at the St. Paul depot in Chicago and met my friends contesting the rights of occupancy with numerous setter-dogs, while all about were shotgun cases and boxes labeled "Ammunition." After greetings I stepped to the station platform and mingled with the crowd—disgusted, and disposed to desert.

A genial young soldier who appreciated the curves in my character followed me out, and explained, in the full flush of his joyous anticipation, that we were going to North Dakota to shoot ducks and prairie chicken, and that it would be the jolliest sort of a time; besides, it was a party of good friends. I hesitated, yielded, and enlisted for the enterprise. Feeling now that I was this far it would be good to go on and learn what there was in the form of sport which charmed so many

A DAKOTA CHICKEN-WAGON

men whose taste I respected in other matters, and once embarked, I summoned my enthusiasm, and tried to "step high, wide, and handsome," as the horsemen say.

True love shall rule

The happiness of a hunting party is like that of a wedding, so important is it that true love shall rule. The *pièce de résistance* of our car was two old generals, who called each other by an abbreviation of their first names, and interrupted conversations by recalling to each other's memory where some acres of men were slain. "A little more of the roast beef, please —yes, that was where I was shot in this side"; and at night, when quiet reigned and we sought sleep, there would be a waving of the curtains, and a voice, "Oh, say, Blank, do you remember that time my horse was hit with the twelve-pounder?" and it banished dreams. There was a phlebotomist from Pittsburgh who had shot all over the earth. He was a thorough sportsman, with a code of rules as complicated as the common-law, and he "made up tough" in his canvas shooting clothes. There was a young and distinguished officer of the regular army who had hunted men, which excused him in the paltry undertaking before him; and, finally, three young men who were adding the accumulated knowledge of Harvard to their natural endowments. For myself, I did not see how jack-boots, spurs, and a Winchester would lend themselves to the

ON THE EDGE OF A SLOUGH

stubble and slough of Dakota, but a collection was taken, and by the time we arrived in Valley City, Dakota, I was armed, if not accoutered, in the style affected by double-barrel men. All I now needed was an education, and between the Doctor, who explained, expostulated, and swore, and a great many "clean misses," I wore on to the high-school stage. Like the obliging person who was asked if he played the violin, I said to myself, "I don't know, but I'll try."

Safety precautions prevent accidents

In the early morning three teams drove up where our car was sidetracked, and we embarked in them. The shotgun man affects buck-colored canvas clothes, with many pockets, and carries his cartridges in his shirt fronts, like a Circassian Cossack. He also takes the shells out of his gun before he climbs into a wagon, or he immediately becomes an object of derision and dread, or, what's worse, suddenly friendless and alone. He also refrains from pointing his gun at any fellow-sportsman, and if he inadvertently does it, he receives a fusillade such as an Irish drill-sergeant throws into a recruit when he does amiss. This day was cool and with a wind blowing, and the poor dogs leaped in delirious joy when let out of their boxes, in which they had traveled all the way from Chicago. After running the wire edge off their nerves they were gotton to range inside a township site, and we jogged along. The first thing which interested me was to hear the Doctor indicate to the driver that he did not care to participate in the driver's knowledge of hunting, and that in order to save mental wear he only had to drive the team, and stand fast when we got out, in order that from the one motionless spot on the prairie sea we could "mark down" the birds.

Endless fields of wheat

The immensity of the wheat fields in Dakota is astonishing to a stranger. They begin on the edge of town, and we drive all day and are never out of them, and on either side they stretch away as far as one's eye can travel. The wheat had been cut and "shocked," which left a stubble some eight inches high. The farmhouses are far apart, and, indeed, not often in sight, but as the threshing was in progress, we saw many groups of men and horses, and the great steam-threshers blowing clouds of black smoke, and the flying straw as it was belched from the bowels of the monsters.

A CONFERENCE IN THE MUD

During the heat of the day the chickens lie in the cover of the grass at the sides of the fields, or in the rank growth of some slough-hole, but at early morning and evening they feed in the wheat stubble. As we ride along, the dogs range out in front, now leaping gracefully along, now stopping and carrying their noses in the air to detect some scent, and finally—"There's a point! Stop, driver!" and we pile out, breaking our guns and shoving in the cartridges.

"I'm a good shooter, but a bad hitter"

"No hurry—no hurry," says the Doctor; "the dog will stay there a month." But, fired with the anticipations, we move briskly up. "You take the right and I'll take the left. Don't fire over the dog," adds the portly sportsman, with an admonishing frown. We go more slowly, and suddenly, with a "whir," up get two chickens and go sailing off. Bang! bang! The Doctor bags his and I miss mine. We load and advance, when up comes the remainder of the covey, and the bewildering plenty of the flying objects rattles me. The Doctor shoots well, indeed prairie chickens are not difficult, but I am discouraged. As the great sportsman Mr. Soapy Sponge used to say, "I'm a good shooter, but a bad hitter." It was in this distressful time that I remembered the words of the old hunter who had charge of my early education in .45 calibres, which ran, "Take yer time, sonny, and always see your hind sight," and by dint of doing this I soon improved to a satisfactory extent. The walking over the stubble is good exercise, and it becomes fascinating to watch the well trained Llewellyn setter "make game," or stand pointing with their tails wagging violently in the nervous thrill of their excitement, then the shooting, and the marking down of the birds who escape the fire, that we may go to them for another "flush." With care and patience one can bag at last the whole covey.

"I am being eaten alive"

At noon we met the other wagons in a green swale, and had lunch, and, seated in a row under the shadow side of a straw stack, we plucked chickens, while the phlebotomist did the necessary surgery to prepare them for the cook. At three o'clock the soldier, a couple of residents, and myself started together for the evening shooting. We banged away at a thousand-yards range at some teal on a big marsh, but later gave it up, and confined ourselves to chicken. In the midst of a covey and a lot of banging I heard the Captain uttering distressful cries. His gun was leaning on a wheat "shock," and he was clawing himself wildly. "Come, help me—I am being eaten alive." Sure enough he was, for in Dakota there is a little insect which is like a winged ant, and they go in swarms, and their bite is sharp and painful. I attempted his rescue, and was attacked in turn, so that we ended by a precipitous retreat, leaving the covey of chickens and their protectors, the ants, on the field.

We next pushed a covey of grouse into some standing oats, and were tempted to go in a short way, but some farmers who were threshing on the neighboring hill blew the engine whistle and made a "sortie," whereat we bolted. At a slough which we were tramping through to kick up some birds "marked down," one suddenly got up under our feet and flew directly over the Captain, who yelled "Don't shoot!" as he dropped to

"DON'T SHOOT!"

the ground. It was a well-considered thing to do, since a flying bird looks bigger than a man to an excited and enthusiastic sportsman. We walked along through the stubble until the red sunset no longer gave sufficient light, and then got into our wagon to do the fourteen miles to our car and supper. Late at night we reached our car, and from it could hear "the sound of revelry." The cook did big Chicago beefsteaks by the half-dozen, for an all day's tramp is a sauce which tells.

"MARK—LEFT"

Duck shooting at Devil's Lake

After some days at this place we were hauled up to Devil's Lake, on the Great Northern road, which locality is without doubt the best for duck-shooting in Dakota. We were driven some sixteen miles to a spur of the lake, where we found a settler. There were hundreds of teal in the water back of his cabin, and as we took position well up the wind and fired, they got up in clouds, and we had five minutes of shooting which was gluttony. We gave the "bag" to the old settler, and the

"MARK !"

Doctor admonished him to "fry them," which I have no doubt he did.

It was six miles to a pond said to be the best evening shooting about there, and we drove over. There we met our other two teams and another party of sportsmen. The shallow water was long and deeply fringed with rank marsh grass. Having no wading-boots can make no difference to a sportsman whose soul is great, so I floundered in and got comfortably wet. After shooting two or three mud-hens, under the impression that they were ducks, the Doctor came along, and with a pained expression he carefully explained what became of people who did not know a teal from a mud-hen, and said further that he would let it pass this time. As the sun sank, the flight of ducks began, and from the far corners of the marsh I saw puffs of smoke and heard the dull slump of a report.

"Mark—left," came a voice from where the young Harvard man with the peach complexion and the cream hair had ensconced himself in the grass, and, sure enough, a flight was coming towards my lair. I waited until it was nearly over, when I rose up and missed two fine shots, while the Harvard man scored. The birds fell well out in the pond, and he waded out to retrieve them.

Teal shooting

As I stood there the soft ooze of the marsh gradually swallowed me, and when in answer to the warning "mark" of my fellows I squatted down in the black water to my middle, and only held my gun and cartridges up, I began to realize that when a teal-duck is coming down wind you have got to aim somewhere into the space ahead of it, hoping to make a connection between your load of shot and the bird. This I did, and after a time got my first birds. The air was now full of flying birds—mallards, spoon-bills, pintails, red-heads, butter-balls, gadwalls, widgeon, and canvas-backs—and the shooting was fast and furious. It was a perfect revelry of slaughter. "Mark—mark." Bang—bang. "What's the matter with that shot?" The sun has set, and no longer bathes the landscape in its golden light, and yet I sit in the water and mud and indulge this pleasurable taste for gore, wondering why it is so ecstatic, or if my companions will not give up shooting presently. There is little probability of that, however. Only darkness can end the miseries of the poor little teal coming home to their marsh, and yet with all my sentimental emotions of sympathy I deplore a miss. If slough-shooting has a drawback, it is its lack of action—it is a calm, deliberate shedding of blood, and a wounding of many birds, who die in the marshes, or become easy prey for the hawks, and it's as cold-blooded as sitting in water can make it.

The end of a perfect day

We give up at last, and the fortunates change their wet clothes, while those who have no change sit on the seat knee-deep in dead birds and shiver while we rattle homeward. Our driver gets himself lost, and we bring up against a wire fence. Very late at night we struck the railroad, and counted telegraph poles and traveled east until the lights of the town twinkled through the gloom. Once in the car, we find the creature comfort which reconciles one to life; and we vote the day a red-letter one. The goose-shooting came later than our visit, but the people tell marvelous tales of their numbers. They employ special guns in their pursuit, which are No. 4 gauge, single-barreled, and very long. They throw buckshot point-blank two hundred yards, and are, indeed, curious-looking arms. The chicken-shooting is not laborious, since one rides in a wagon, and a one-lunged, wooden-legged man is as good as a four-mile athlete at it. He must know setter-dogs, who

TROOPING HOMEWARD IN THE AFTER-GLOW

are nearly as complicated as women in their temper and ways; he must have a nose for cover, and he can be taught to shoot; he can keep statistics if he desires; but his first few experiences behind the dogs will not tempt him to do that unless his modesty is highly developed. If he become a shotgun enthusiast he will discover a most surprising number of fellows—doctors, lawyers, butchers, farmers, and Indians not taxed—all willing to go with him or to be interested in his tales.

The car was to be attached to an express train bound west that night, to my intense satisfaction, and I crawled into the upper berth to dream of bad-lands elk, soldiers, cowboys, and only in the haze of fleeting consciousness could I distinguish a voice—

"Remington, I hope you are not going to fall out of that upper berth again tonight."

I Found No Strangers

by John Steinbeck from *Travels with Charley In Search of America*

It would be pleasant to be able to say of my travels with Charley, "I went out to find the truth about my country and I found it." And then it would be such a simple matter to set down my findings and lean back comfortably with a fine sense of having discovered truths and taught them to my readers. I wish it were that easy. But what I carried in my head and deeper in my perceptions was a barrel of worms. I discovered long ago in collecting and classifying marine animals that what I found was closely intermeshed with how I felt at the moment. External reality has a way of being not so external after all.

This monster of a land, this mightiest of nations, this spawn of the future, turns out to be the macrocosm of microcosm me. If an Englishman or a Frenchman or an Italian should travel my route, see what I saw, hear what I heard, their stored pictures would be not only different from mine but equally different from one another. If other Americans reading this account should feel it true, that agreement would only mean that we are alike in our Americanness.

From start to finish I found no strangers. If I had, I might be able to report them more objectively. But these are my people and this my country. If I found matters to criticize and to deplore, they were tendencies equally present in myself. If I were to prepare one immaculately inspected generality it would be this: For all of our enormous geographic range, for all of our sectionalism, for all of our interwoven breeds drawn from every part of the ethnic world, we are a nation, a new breed. Americans are much more American than they are Northerners, Southerners, Westerners, or Easterners. And descendants of English, Irish, Italian, Jewish, German, Polish are essentially American. This is not patriotic whoop-de-do; it is carefully observed fact. California Chinese, Boston Irish, Wisconsin German, yes, and Alabama Negroes, have more in common than they have apart. And this is the more remarkable because it has happened so quickly. It is a fact that Americans from all sections and of all racial extractions are more alike than the Welsh are like the English, the Lancashireman like the Cockney, or for that matter the Lowland Scot like the Highlander. It is astonishing that this has happened in less than two hundred years and most of it in the last fifty. The American identity is an exact and provable thing.

Yanks 1917-1918

by James W. Foley

O'Leary, from Chicago, and a first-class fightin' man,
For his father was from Kerry, where the gentle art began:
Sergeant Dennis P. O'Leary, from somewhere on Archie Road,
Dodgin' shells and smellin' powder while the battle ebbed and flowed.

And the captain says: "O'Leary, from your fightin' company
Pick a dozen fightin' Yankees and come skirmishin' with me;
Pick a dozen fightin' devils, and I know it's you who can."
And O'Leary, he saluted like a first-class fightin' man.

O'Leary's eye was piercin' and O'Leary's voice was clear:
"Dimitri Georgoupoulos!" And Dimitri answered "Here!"
Then "Vladimir Slaminsky! Step three paces to the front,
For we're wantin' you to join us in a little Heinie hunt!"

"Garibaldi Ravioli!" Garibaldi was to share;
And "Ole Axel Kettleson!" and "Thomas Scalp-the-Bear!"
Who was Choctaw by inheritance, bred in the blood and bones,
But set down in army records by the name of Thomas Jones.

"Van Winkle Schuyler Stuyvesant!" Van Winkle was a bud
From the ancient tree of Stuyvesant and had it in his blood;
"Don Miguel de Colombo!" Don Miguel's next of kin
Were across the Rio Grande when Don Miguel went in.

"Ulysses Grant O'Sheridan!" Ulysses' sire, you see,
Had been at Appomattox near the famous apple-tree;
And "Patrick Michael Casey!" Patrick Michael, you can tell,
Was a fightin' man by nature with three fightin' names as well.

"Joe Wheeler Lee!" And Joseph had a pair of fightin' eyes;
And his granddad was a Johnny, as perhaps you might surmise;
Then "Robert Bruce MacPherson!" And the Yankee squad was done
With "Isaac Abie Cohen!" once a lightweight champion.

Then O'Leary paced 'em forward and, says he: "You Yanks, fall in!"
And he marched 'em to the captain. "Let the skirmishin' begin."
Says he, "The Yanks are comin', and you beat 'em if you can!"
And saluted like a soldier and first-class fightin' man!

"I propose to treat you fairly and squarely!"

Observations by Marcus Aurelius

How strangely men act! Some are unwilling to speak well of their contemporaries, and yet are very anxious to be praised by posterity, whom they have never seen nor will see. This is about as foolish as to be vexed that we cannot obtain the praises of our ancestors.

* * * * *

If anything seems exceedingly difficult to you, do not conclude that it is beyond human power. Think, rather, that whatever is possible to man, and right for him to do, is within your reach.

* * * * *

If, in gymnastic exercises, someone scratches us with his nails or bruises us accidentally on the head, we do not protest, nor get angry, nor thereafter suspect that the injury was designed. And yet we are on our guard against him, not with hostility or suspicion, but with a good-natured caution for our own safety. Let it be so in the rest of life: let us look on many other things as on these accidents of the games. We must, as I said, be upon our guard, but without suspicion or enmity.

* * * * *

If anyone can show me and convince me that I am wrong in thought or deed, I will gladly change. I am seeking the truth, by which no one is ever hurt. But one is hurt by remaining in self-deception and ignorance.

* * * * *

I do my duty; other things give me no concern; they are either soulless or reasonless, or misguided and ignorant of the right way.

* * * * *

How stale and insincere this sounds: "I propose to treat you fairly and squarely!" Why this to-do, man? What is the need of protestation? The truth will soon be found out. Such a profession should be written on your forehead. One should see your honesty shining in your eyes, as a lover discerns affection in the eyes of his beloved. Simple and straightforward goodness should be like a strong perfume, instantly perceived by one who draws near its source, whether he will or not.

Qualities That Earn Respect

From *The Meditations of Marcus Aurelius*

After enumerating certain basic values which he had acquired from various individuals who influenced his life, he described his father as follows:

From my father—

Gentleness and unwavering adherence to judgments formed after due deliberation.

Indifference to honors, commonly so called.

Industry and assiduity.

Readiness to listen to any scheme for promoting the common good.

An inflexible determination to render every man his due.

Tact to choose the proper time for severity and for leniency.

Suppression of unnatural lusts.

A sense of fellowship with mankind.

His friends might absent themselves altogether from his table, or fail to attend him in public, if they were so inclined; and he never thought less of them on this account. He was exact and patient in all official inquiries and deliberations, never quitting the search, and never satisfied with first appearances.

Zealous to retain his friends, he was never sentimental or foolishly fond. In every situation he was contented, cheery, thoughtful of the future, and careful about small matters, without fussiness. Acclamations and flattery he repressed. The resources of the government were carefully husbanded, and the public revenues economically expended, and no attention was paid to the censures occasioned by this prudence.

Toward the gods he was not superstitious, nor toward men demagogical, obsequious, or studious of popularity; but sober in all things, steadfast, an enemy of vulgarity and mere novelty. The conveniences and comforts of life, which fortune gave him in abundance, he used without arrogance, yet freely, enjoying them sincerely when he had them, and not missing them when they were lacking. No one could accuse him of sophistry, vulgarity, or pedantry. He was a mature, well-rounded man, intolerant of flattery, and able to govern both himself and others.

Notable also was the great honor he paid to all true philosophers, without upbraiding those who were not so, or being led astray by them. In conversation he was gracious and charming, though a moderate talker. Of his body he took proper care, but not like one anxious for length of life, avoiding the extremes of foppishness and slovenliness. As a result of this care, he seldom had need of the physician, and made little use of medicines and embrocations.

Perhaps his most striking characteristic was his readiness to yield, without envy, to those who had attained especial proficiency in oratory, jurisprudence, the knowledge of ancient customs, or in any other matter, and he was eager to promote their reputation. Always patriotic in his actions, he made no parade of such matters.

"Nothing natural can be evil."

by MARCUS AURELIUS

The lifetime of man is but a point; his being a flux; his perceptions faint and dull; his physical organism corruptible; his soul a vortex; his destiny inscrutable; and his fame uncertain. In brief, his bodily existence is an ever-flowing stream; that of his soul, a dream and a vapor. His life is a warfare and a sojourn in a strange land, and his after-fame oblivion.

What, then, can be our guide? Philosophy alone. And this consists in keeping the divinity within us inviolate; superior to pleasures and pains; free from inconsiderateness in action, and insincerity and hypocrisy; independent of what others may do or leave undone; accepting cheerfully whatever befalls or is appointed, as coming from the same source as himself; and, above all, awaiting death with a serene mind, as the natural dissolution of the elements of which every animal is compounded.

And if for the elements there is nothing terrible in the continual change from one form into another, why should one dread the transformation and dissolution of the whole? It is natural, and nothing natural can be evil.

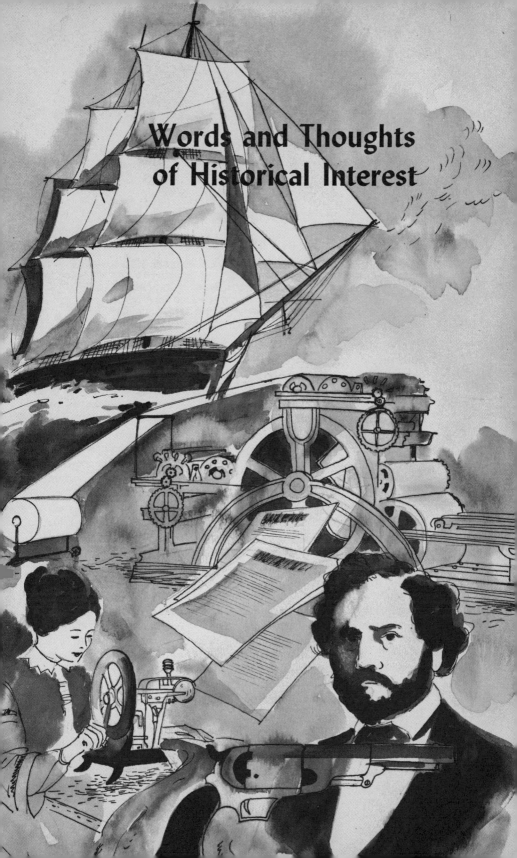

Words and Thoughts
of Historical Interest

The Barber

From *The Every-Day Book*, an almanac for 1826, by WILLIAM HONE

*Since the revival of interest in the styles of beards
and unusual hair styles, including the use of wigs,
this article has considerably more relevance today
than would have been true five years ago.*

Randle Holme, an indisputable authority, in his great work on heraldry figures a barber as above—"a barber bare-headed with a pair of scissors in his right hand and a comb in his left, clothed in russet, his apron checked in russet and azure. A barber is always known by his checked, party-colored apron; therefore, it needs not mentioning."

Holme emphatically adds, "Neither can he be termed a barber (or poller or shaver, as anciently they were called), till his apron be about him; that is to say, his checked party-colored apron." This, and this only, is the "flag of his profession."

Holme derives the denomination barber from *barba*, a beard, and describes him as a cutter of hair. He was also anciently termed a poller because in former times to poll was to cut the hair—to trim was to cut the beard, after shaving, into form and order.

*   *   *

The instrument-case of a barber and the instruments in their several divisions are particularly described by Holme. The case contained his looking glass, a set of horn combs with teeth on one side, and wide—"for the combing and readying of long, thick, and stony heads of hair, and such like periwigs," a set of box combs, a set of ivory combs with fine teeth on both sides, an ivory beard-comb, a beard-iron called the forceps, being a curling iron for the beard, a set of razors, tweezers with an ear-pick, a rasp to file the point of a tooth, a hone for his razors, a bottle of sweet oil for his hone, a powder box with sweet powder, a puff to powder the hair, a four square bottle with a screwed head for sweet water, wash balls and sweet balls, caps for the head to keep the hair up, trimming cloths to put before a man, and napkins to put about his neck and dry his hands and face with.

After he was shaved and barbed, the barber was to hold him the glass, that he might see "his new-made face," and instruct the barber where it was amiss: the barber was then to "take off the linens, brush his clothes, present him with his hat, and, according to his hire, make a bow, with 'your humble servant, sir.' "

The same author thus figures

The Barber's Candlestick

He describes it to be "a wooden turned stick, having a socket in the straight piece, and another in the cross or overthwart piece; this he sticketh in his apron strings on his left side or breast when he frequently trims by candlelight."

Without going into every particular concerning the utensils and art of "barbing and shaving," some may be deemed curious, and therefore worthy of notice. It is to be observed, however, that they are from Randle Holme, who wrote in 1688, and relate to barbers of former days.

Barber's Basin

The barber's washing or trimming basin had a circle in the brim to compass a man's throat, and a place like a little dish to put the ball in after lathering. Holme says, "Such a like basin as this valiant Don Quixote took from a bloody enchanting barber, which he took to be a golden headpiece."

The barber's basin is very ancient; it is mentioned by Ezekiel the prophet. In the Middle Ages it was of bright copper.

Razor

This is a figure of the old razor of a superior kind, tipped with silver. "That is," says Holme, "silver plates engraven are fixed upon each end of the haft, to make the same look more genteel and rich." The old man, being fidgetted by this ornament, declares, "It is very oft done by young, proud artists who adorn their instruments with silver shrines, more than setting themselves forth by the glory that attends their art, or praise obtained by skill."

Before English manufacturers excelled in cutlery, razors were imported from Palermo. Razors are mentioned by Homer.

Barber's Chafer

"This is a small chafer which they use to carry about with them, when they make any progress to trim or barb gentlemen at a distance, to carry their sweet water (or countryman's broth) in; the

round handle at the mouth of the chafer is to fall down as soon as their hand leaves it," says Holme.

Mr. J. T. Smith remarks that "the 'flying barber' is a character now no more to be seen in London, though he still remains in some of our country villages. He was provided with a napkin, soap, and pewter basin, the form of which may be seen in many of the illustrative prints of Don Quixote." The same writer speaks of the barber's chafer as being "a deep, leaden vessel, something like a chocolate pot, with a large ring, or handle, at the top. This pot held about a quart of water boiling hot, and thus equipped, he flew about to his customers."

These chafers are no longer made in London. The last mold which produced them was sold in New Street, Shoe Lane, at the sale of Mr. Richard Joseph's molds for pewter utensils in January, 1815. It was of brass and broken up for metal.

Barber's Chafing Dish

This was a metal firepot, with a turning handle, and much used during winter, especially in shops without fireplaces. It was carried by the handle from place to place, but generally set under a brass or copper basin with a flat, broad bottom, whereon, if linen cloths were rubbed or let remain, they in a little time became hot or warm for the barber's use.

Barber's Crisping Irons

This is their ancient shape. "In former times these were much used to curl the side locks of a man's head, but now (in 1688) wholly

cast aside as useless; it openeth and shutteth like the forceps, only the ends are broad and square, being cut within the mouth with teeth curled and crisped, one tooth striking within another."

Scissors

Hair-scissors were long and broad in the blades, and rounded toward the points, which were sharp.

Beard-scissors had short blades and long handles.

The barber's scissors differed in these respects from others. For instance, the tailor's scissors had blunt points, while the seamster's scissors differed from both by reason of their smallness, some of them having one ring for the thumb only to fit it, while the contrary ring or bow was large enough to admit two or three fingers.

Beards

Pick-a-devant Beard

A full face with a sharp pointed beard is termed, in recorded descriptions, a man's face with a "pick-a-devant (or sharp pointed) beard."

Mr. Archdeacon Nares' *Glossary* contains several passages in corroboration of Holme's description of this beard.

Cathedral Beard

This Holme calls "the broad or cathedral beard, because bishops and grave men of the church anciently did wear such beards." Besides this and the "pick-a-devant" he says there are several sorts and fashions of beards. "The British beard hath long mustachios on the higher lip, hanging down either side of the chin, all the rest of the face being bare. The forked beard is a broad beard ending in two points. The mouse-eaten beard, when the beard groweth scatteringly, not together, but here a tuft and there a tuft."

Guillaume Duprat, Bishop of Clermont, who assisted at the Council of Trent, and built the college of the Jesuits at Paris, had the finest beard that ever was seen. It was too fine a beard for a bishop, and the canons of his cathedral, in full chapter assembled, came to the barbarous resolution of shaving him. Accordingly, when next he came to the choir, the dean, the provost, and the choirmaster approached with scissors and razors, soap, basin and warm water. He took to his heels at the sight and escaped to his castle of Beauregard, about two leagues from Clermont, where he fell sick of vexation, and died.

Ancient monuments represent the Greek heroes to have worn short, curled beards. Among the Romans, after the year 454, B.C., philosophers alone constantly wore a beard. The beard of their military men was short and frizzed. The first emperors with a long and thick beard were—Hadrian, who wore it to hide his wounds, and Antoninus Pius and Marcus Aurelius, who wore it as philosophers. A thick beard was afterwards considered an appendage that attained for the emperors veneration from the people.

Wigs

A Peruke

It is figured as seen above by Holme, who also calls it, in his peculiar orthography, a "perawick," and says it was likewise called "short bob, a head of hair—a wig that hath short locks and a hairy crown." He describes it with some feeling. "This is counterfeit hair, which men wear instead of their own—a thing much used in our days by the generality of men, contrary to our forefathers, who got estates, loved their wives, and wore their own hair—but in these days (1688) there are no such things!"

He further gives the following as

A Long Periwig, with a Pole-Lock

This he puts forth as being by artists called "a long, curled wig with a *dildo* [cylindrical or sausage curl], or pole-lock." And he affirms that this is the sign or cognizance of the "perawick-maker."

That the peruke was anciently a barber's sign is verified by a very rare, and perhaps unique, engraving of St. Paul's Cathedral when being built, with the scaffolding poles and boards up.

This print, in the possession of the editor of the *Every-Day Book,* represents a barber's shop on the north side of St. Paul's churchyard, with a barber's pole out at the door, and a swinging sign projecting from each side of the house, a peruke being painted on each.

A Traveling Wig

This peruke, with a curled foretop and bobs, was a kind of traveling wig, having the side or bottom locks turned up into "bobs or knots tied with ribbons." Holme further calls it "a campaign wig," and says, "It hath knots or bobs, or a dildo, on each side, with a curled forehead."

A Grafted Wig

is described by Holme as "a perawick with a turn on the top of the head, in imitation of a man's hairy crown."

A Border of Hair

This is so called by Holme; he also calls it "a peruke with the crown or top cut off; some term it

the border of a peruke." He adds, "Women usually wear such borders, which they call curls or locks when they hang over their ears." He further says they were called "taures" when set in curls on the forehead, and "merkins" when the curls were worn lower, or at the sides of the face.

A Bull-Head

"Some," says Holme, "term this curled forehead a bull-head, from the French word 'taure,' because 'taure' is a bull. It was the fashion of women to wear bull-heads, or bull-like foreheads, anno 1674, and about that time; this is the coat of arms of Taurell, a French lord."

Curls on Wires

According to our chief authority, Holme, a female thus coiffed, with "a pair of locks and curls," was in great fashion about the year 1670. He adds that they are "false locks, set on wires, to make them stand at a distance from the head—as the farthingales made their clothes stand out, from the hips downwards, in Queen Elizabeth's reign."

Female Headdress in 1688

There is a little difficulty in naming this headdress, for Holme is so diffuse and indignant that he gives it no term though he describes the engraving. The figure is remarkable because it is in many respects similar to the manner wherein the ladies of 1825 adjust the head. It will be remembered that Holme was a herald, and though his descriptions have not hitherto been here related in his armorial language, he always sets them out so in his "storehouse of armory and blazon." It may be amusing to conclude these extracts from him with his description of this figure in his own words. Thus then the old "deputy for the kings of arms" describes it:

"A woman's face, her forehead adorned with a knot of diverse colored ribbons—the head, with a ruffled coif set in corners—and the like ribbons behind the head. This is a fashionmonger's head, tricked and trimmed up, according to the mode of these times wherein I am writing of it; and, in my judgment, were a fit 'coat' for such seamsters as are skilled in inventions. But why do I talk of 'arms' to such, by reason they will be shortly old, and therefore not to be endured by them whose brains are always upon new devices and inventions? But all are brought again from the old, for there is no new thing under the sun —for what is now hath been formerly!"

My Fancy

From *College Rhymes* by LEWIS CARROLL

I painted her a gushing thing,
   With years perhaps a score;
I little thought to find they were
   At least a dozen more;
My fancy gave her eyes of blue,
   A curly auburn head:
I came to find the blue a green,
   The auburn turned to red.

She boxed my ears this morning,
   They tingled very much;
I own that I could wish her
   A somewhat lighter touch;

And if you were to ask me how
   Her charms might be improved,
I would not have them *added to*,
   But just a few *removed!*

She has the bear's ethereal grace,
   The bland hyena's laugh,
The footstep of the elephant,
   The neck of the giraffe;
I love her still, believe me,
   Though my heart its passion hides;
"She's all my fancy painted her,"
   But oh! *how much besides!*

Reflect Upon the Limitless Expanse of Time

by Marcus Aurelius

Let nothing be done at random, but according to the perfect rules of art.

* * * * *

Men seek retirement in country houses, at the seashore, or in the mountains. You, too, used to long for it. But it is the simplest thing in the world, for at any hour you please you may retire into yourself. Nowhere can man live in seclusion more calm and uninterrupted than that of his own soul, especially if it is so furnished that when he looks about him he is straightway perfectly at ease.

Does the little matter of fame disturb you? Reflect upon the swift oblivion of all things; the limitless expanse of time that lies on either side of you; the hollowness of the echo of applause; the fickleness and senselessness of the applauders; the narrowness of the bounds by which you are circumscribed.

The whole earth is only a point, and your dwelling-place but a little corner of it; and how few there are upon it to praise us, and how little they are worth!

Be thou free, and regard things as a man, as one among men, as a citizen, as a mortal.

* * * * *

If intelligence is common to us all, so is that reason by virtue of which we are rational beings. But if so, then is that practical reason which tells us what should be done, and what not done, a common possession. It follows that we all have a common law, that we are all fellow-citizens under one common government, and that our commonwealth is the world. For of what other citizenship can all men be said to be partakers?

Thence—from this common citizenship—we have our intelligence, our reason, our law. If not, whence come they? For just as the earthy in me is derived from earth, the watery from some other element, the aerial from some special source, and the warm or fiery also from its proper fountain,—for nothing can arise from nothing, or return into it,—so likewise must the spiritual in me surely have an origin of its own.

***

The Choice
by Edmund Vance Cooke

The little it takes to make life bright,
  If we open our eyes to get it!
And the trifle which makes it black as night,
  If we close our lids and let it!
Behold, as the world goes whirling by,
It is gloomy, or glad, as it fits your eye.

As it fits your eye, and I mean by that
  You find what you look for mostly;
You can feed your happiness full and fat,
  You can make your miseries ghostly,
Or you can forget every joy you own
By coveting something beyond your zone.

In the storms of life we can fret the eye
  Where the guttering mud is drifted,
Or we can look to the world-wide sky
  Where the Artist's scenes are shifted.
Puddles are oceans in miniatures,
Or merely puddles; the choice is yours.

We can strip our niggardly souls so bare
  That we haggle a penny between us;
Or we can be rich in a common share
  Of the Pleiades and Venus.
You can lift your soul to its outermost look,
Or can keep it packed in a pocketbook.

We may follow a phantom the arid miles
  To a mountain of cankered treasure,
Or we can find, in a baby's smiles,
  The pulse of a living pleasure.
We may drink of the sea until we burst,
While the trickling spring would have quenched
        our thirst.

* * *

American Individualism

by HERBERT HOOVER

My faith in the essential truth, strength and vitality of the developing creed, by which we have hitherto lived in this country of ours, has been confirmed and deepened by the searching experiences of seven years of service in the backwash and misery of war. From it all I emerge an individualist, an American individualist, for America has been steadily developing the ideals that constitute progressive individualism.

Our individualism differs from all others because it embraces the following great ideals: that while we build our society upon the attainment of the individual, we shall safeguard to every individual an equality of opportunity to take that position in the community to which his intelligence, character, ability and ambition entitle him; that we keep the social solution free from frozen strata of classes; that we shall stimulate effort of each individual to achievement; that through an enlarging sense of responsibility and understanding, we shall assist him to this attainment; while he, in turn, must stand up to the emery wheel of competition.

We in America have had too much experience of life to fool ourselves into pretending that all men are equal in ability, in character, in intelligence, in ambition. That was part of the claptrap of the French Revolution. We have grown to understand that all we can hope to assure to the individual, through government, is liberty, justice, intellectual welfare, equality of opportunity and stimulation to service. Humanity has a long road to perfection, but we of America can make sure progress if we will preserve and stimulate the initiative of our people, if we will build up our safeguards to equality of opportunity, if we will glorify service as a part of our national character. Progress will march if we hold an abiding faith in the intelligence, the initiative, the character, the courage and the divine touch in the individual.

*　　*　　*　　*　　*

The dangers of America are not economic or foreign foes; they are moral and spiritual. Social and moral and spiritual values outrank economic values. Economic gains, even scientific gains, are worse than useless if they accrue to a people unfitted by trained character to use and not abuse them.

— *Herbert Hoover*

One of Benjamin Franklin's unique publishing
ventures—a guide to the improvement of one's
financial condition in the form of a rebus.

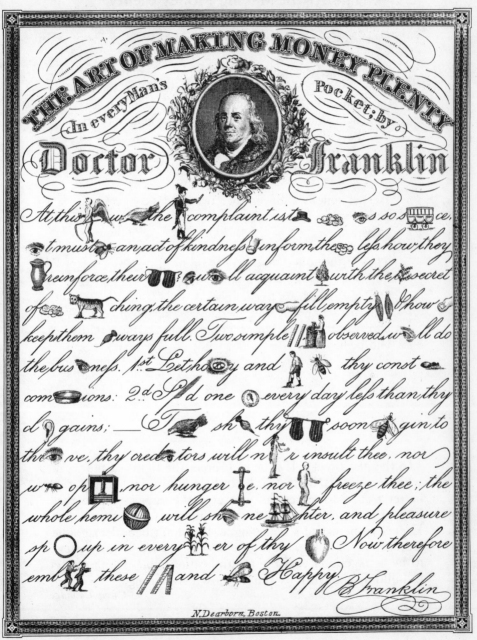

The Art of Making Money Plenty

A translation of Benjamin Franklin's animated poster appearing on the preceding page.

At this time when the general complaint is that money is so scarce, it must be an act of kindness to inform the moneyless how they can reinforce their pouches. I will acquaint you with the true secret of money catching, the certain way to fill empty pockets and how to keep them always full. Two simple rules well observed will do the business.

1st. Let honesty and work be thy constant companions. 2nd. Spend one penny every day less than thy clear gains.

Then shall thy pouches soon begin to thrive, thy creditors will never insult thee, nor want oppress, nor hunger bite, nor nakedness freeze thee: the whole hemisphere will shine brighter, and pleasure spring up in every corner of thy heart. Now therefore embrace these rules and be happy.

B. Franklin

Do the day's work. If it be to protect the rights of the weak, whoever objects, do it. If it be to help a powerful corporation better to serve the people, whatever the opposition, do that. Expect to be called a standpatter, but don't be a standpatter. Expect to be called a demagogue, but don't be a demagogue. Don't hesitate to be as revolutionary as science. Don't hesitate to be as reactionary as the multiplication table. Don't expect to build up the weak by pulling down the strong.

—*Calvin Coolidge*

An Informal Visit with Benjamin Franklin

From *The Table-Talk and Bon-Mots of Samuel Foote*—1889
Edited by WILLIAM COOKE

The celebrated philosopher, Dr. Benjamin Franklin, though very different in general temper and habits, was not unknown to Foote and his junto, whose wit he often relished as a seasoning to deeper thoughts and graver studies.

The Doctor, speaking of those early and accidental inducements which lead the mind to particular arts or sciences, gave another testimony to the opinion of Dr. Johnson and others that "he who would perfect his style should turn over the pages of Addison by day and by night." It was by stumbling accidentally, he said, on an odd volume of the *Spectator*, when a boy, that he was first induced to become a reader, and afterwards a writer. His method, which is given here as no inconsiderable example, was as follows:

"I was delighted," said he, "with the style of the *Spectator* and was desirous, if possible, to imitate it. In order to succeed, I selected some of the papers, made short summaries of the sense of each period, and laid them aside for some days; after which I endeavored, without looking at the original, to recompose the essay; and to express at length each thought as it was in the book, employing only such phrases as occurred to my own mind."

By degrees this plan succeeded, and though he lacked the finished graces of an Addisonian style (and who has been able to catch them?) he acquired a familiarity of expression and a correctness of thinking which perhaps without this aid he would never have been able to attain.

Swift had strength and precision, Dryden often united elegance to strength, and Bolingbroke was happy in both; but Addison had a grace in writing, with such a well-bred familiarity in expression, independent of his judgment as a critic and a moralist, as rendered him unique among English writers.

* * * * *

Dr. Franklin once examining a boy at the request of his father, relative to the progress he had made in his learning, found him offering excuses for almost everything which he should have done. This he listened to for some time with great patience, and very much to the boy's satisfaction, who thought he had deceived him. At last he said, in his usual grave manner: "I grant you, young gentleman, you have been very ingenious in your apologies for not doing your duty, and as such I must report you to your father; but this I must likewise tell him as well as you—that the boy who is good at excuses is generally good for nothing else."

*　*　*　*　*

When people who had got together a little money in trade used to be capriciously wishing to live in the country (without having a single quality or habit to fit them for agriculture, its pursuit, or enjoyments), he would dryly ask, "What do you think of the country for?"

The answer usually was, "Oh, because I am tired of the town."

"And for this reason," replied he, "you want to *re-tire* in the country."

*　*　*　*　*

On the subject of natural and artificial education, he used to tell the following anecdote:

On the conclusion of some treaty between a party of Indians with the Council of Pennsylvania, the latter offered to the former to educate some of their young men according to the modes of civilized life. The Indians, after duly considering the proposal, declined the offer, asking at the same time, "What can we get by the exchange of education? You cannot walk so fast, nor so well, as we can. You cannot fight so well, nor are you such good marksmen. Our wants are fewer, our distinctions less, without jealousy, ambition, etc. But as you mean to live friendly with us, we are ready to communicate *these blessings* to you, by educating, from time to time, a number of the young men of your nation."

*　*　*　*　*

When he heard people say they were "tired of a thing," merely through a want of proper perseverance, he used to reply, "Well, do as married people do—tire and begin again."

*　*　*　*　*

Franklin's father was a Puritan of the old stamp, and with other peculiarities of this sect, was accustomed to precede all his meals with long prayers, and sometimes to say grace over every particular dish. This not agreeing with the impatience of young Franklin's appetite, who was then about eleven years old, he determined to give his father a broad hint. Accordingly, when, at the beginning of winter he was, as usual, busy in salting provisions for the season, he asked his father whether it would not be better to crave a blessing, once for all, on the whole cask of provisions, then, as it would be a wonderful saving of time in the future.

*   *   *   *   *

His peculiar talent was that of illustrating subjects by appropriate anecdotes. When he was agent here for the province of Pennsylvania, he was frequently applied to by the ministry for his opinion respecting the operation of the *Stamp Act*, but his answer was uniformly the same, that "the people of America would never submit to it."

After the news of the destruction of the stamped papers had arrived in England, the ministry again sent for the Doctor to consult with, and in conclusion offered the proposal that "if the Americans would engage to pay for the damage done in the destruction of the stamped paper, etc., the Parliament would then repeal the Act."

The Doctor, having paused upon this question for some time, at last answered it as follows:

"This puts me in mind of a Frenchman, who, having heated a poker red-hot, ran furiously into the street, addressing the first Englishman he met there: '*Hah! Monsieur, voulez-vous* give me *de plaisir, de satisfaction*, to let me run this poker only one foot into your body?'

" 'My body!' replied the Englishman. 'What do you mean?'

" '*Vel den*, only so far," marking about six inches.

" 'Are you mad?' returned the other. 'I tell you, if you don't go about your business, I'll knock you down.'

" '*Vel den*,' said the Frenchman, softening his voice and manner, '*vil* you, my good sire, only be so obliging as to pay me for the trouble and expense of heating this poker?' "

*   *   *   *   *

When anyone was for proving the fortune and respectability of another by the number of servants, carriages, etc., the Doctor used to reply, "Well, well. This may be your opinion, and the opinion of many people, but I have not yet learned that extravagance is the criterion of fortune or independence."

Thomas Paine Speculates about the Future of America

From a letter to George Washington written in Paris in 1796

Soon after the Federal Constitution arrived in England, I received a letter from a female literary correspondent (a native of New York) very well mixed with friendship, sentiment, and politics. In my answer to that letter I permitted myself to ramble into the wilderness of imagination, and to anticipate what might hereafter be the condition of America.

I had no idea that the picture I then drew was realizing so fast, and still less, that Mr. Washington was hurrying it on. As the extract I allude to is pertinent to the subject I am upon, I hereby transcribe it.

"You touch me on a very tender point when you say that my friends on your side of the water cannot be reconciled to the idea of my abandoning America, even for my native England. They are right. I would rather see my horse Button eating the grass of Bordentown or Morrisenia than see all the pomp and show of Europe.

"A thousand years hence—for I must indulge a few thoughts —perhaps in less time, America may be what England now is. The innocence of her character, that won the hearts of all nations in her favor, may sound like a romance, and her inimitable virtue, as if it had never been.

"The ruins of that liberty which thousands bled to obtain may just furnish material for a village tale, or extort a sigh from rustic sensibility; while the fashionable of that day, enveloped in dissipation, shall deride the principle and deny the fact.

"When we contemplate the fall of empires and the extinction of the nations of the ancient world, we see but little more to excite our regret than the moldering ruins of pompous palaces, magnificent monuments, lofty pyramids, and walls and towers of the most costly workmanship. But when the empire of America shall fall, the subject for contemplative sorrow will be infinitely greater than crumbling brass or marble can inspire.

"It will not then be said, here stood a temple of vast antiquity, here rose a babel of invisible height, or there a palace of sumptuous extravagance; but here—ah painful thought!—the noblest work of human wisdom, the grandest scene of human glory, the fair cause of freedom rose and fell.

"Read this, and then ask if I forget America!"

Lafayette's First Visit to America

by GEORGE TICKNOR from *The Percy Anecdotes*
to which is added a valuable collection of *American Anecdotes*

When only between sixteen and seventeen, Lafayette was married to the daughter of the Duke d'Ayen, son of the Duke de Noailles and grandson to the great and good Chancellor d'Aguesseau; and thus his condition in life seemed to be assured to him among the most splendid and powerful in the empire.

His fortune, which had been accumulating during a long minority, was vast; his rank was with the first in Europe; his connections brought him the support of the chief persons in France; and his individual character—the warm, open and sincere manners, which have distinguished him ever since, and given him such singular control over the minds of men—made him powerful in the confidence of society wherever he went. It seemed, indeed, as if life had nothing further to offer him than he could surely obtain by walking in the path that was so bright before him.

It was at this period, however, that his thoughts and feelings were first turned towards these thirteen colonies, then in the darkest and most doubtful passage of their struggle for independence. He made himself acquainted with our agents at Paris, and learned from them the state of our affairs.

Nothing could be less tempting to him, whether he sought military reputation or military instruction; for our army, at that moment retreating through New Jersey, and leaving its traces of blood from the naked and torn feet of the soldiery, as it hastened onward, was in a state too humble to offer either. Our credit, too, in Europe was entirely gone, so that the commissioners (as they were called, without having any commission), to whom Lafayette still persisted in offering his services, were obliged, at last, to acknowledge that they could not even give him decent means for his conveyance.

"Then," said he, "I shall purchase and fit out a vessel for myself." He did so. The vessel was prepared at Bordeaux, and sent round to one of the nearest ports in Spain, that it might be beyond the reach of the French government. In order more effectually to conceal his purposes, he made, just before his embarkation, a visit of a few weeks in England—the only time he was ever there—and was much sought in English society. On his return to France, he did not stop at all in the capital, even to see his own family, but hastened with all speed and secrecy to make good his escape from the country. It was not until he was thus on his way to embark that his romantic undertaking began to be known.

The effect produced in the capital and at court by its publication was greater than we should now perhaps imagine. Lord Stormont, the English ambassador, required the French ministry to dispatch an order for his arrest, not only to Bordeaux, but to the French commanders on the West India station— a requisition with which the ministry readily complied, for they were at that time anxious to preserve a good understanding with England, and were seriously angry with a young man who had thus put in jeopardy the relations of the two countries. In fact, at Passage, on the very borders of France and Spain a *lettre de cachet* overtook him, and he was arrested and carried back to Bordeaux.

There, of course, his enterprise was near being finally stopped; but, watching his opportunity, and assisted by one or two friends, he disguised himself as a courier, with his face blacked and false hair, and rode on, ordering post horses for the carriage which he had caused to follow him at a suitable distance for this very purpose, and thus fairly passed the frontiers of the two kingdoms only three or four hours before his pursuers reached them. He soon arrived at the port where his vessel was waiting for him. His family, however, still followed him with solicitations to return, which he never received; and the society of the court and capital, according to Madame du Deffand's account of it, was in no common state of excitement on the occasion.

Something of the same sort happened in London. "We talk chiefly," said Gibbon in a letter dated April 12, 1777, "of the Marquis de Lafayette, who was here a few weeks ago. He is about twenty, with a hundred and thirty thousand pounds a year—the nephew of Noailles, who is ambassador here. He has bought the Duke of Kingston's yacht [a mistake], and has gone to join the Americans. The court appears to be angry with him."

Immediately on arriving the second time at Passage, the wind being fair, he embarked. The usual course for French vessels attempting to trade with our colonies at that period was to sail for the West Indies, and then, coming up along our coast, enter where they could. But this course would have exposed Lafayette to the naval commanders of his own nation, and he had almost as much reason to dread them as to dread British cruisers.

When, therefore, they were outside of the Canary Islands, Lafayette required his captain to lay their course directly for the United States. The captain refused, alleging that, if they should be taken by a British force and carried into Halifax, the French government would never reclaim them, and they could hope for nothing but a slow death in a dungeon or a prison-ship. This was true, but Lafayette knew it before he made the requisition. He therefore insisted, until the captain refused in the most positive manner. Lafayette then told him that the ship was his own private property, that he had made his own arrangements concerning it, and that if he, the captain, would not sail directly for the United States, he should be put in irons and his command given to the next officer. The captain, of course, submitted, and Lafayette gave him a bond for forty thousand francs, in case of any accident.

They therefore now made sail directly for the southern portion of the United States and arrived unmolested at Charleston, South Carolina, on the 25th of April, 1777.

The sensation produced by his appearance in this country was, of course, much greater than that produced in Europe by his departure. It still stands forth as one of the most prominent and important circumstances in our revolutionary contest; and, as has often been said by one who bore no small part in its trials and success, none but those who were then alive can believe what an impulse it gave to the hopes of a population almost disheartened by a long series of disasters. And well it might, for it taught us that in the first rank of the first nobility in Europe, men could still be found who not only took an interest in our struggle but were willing to share our sufferings; that our obscure and almost desperate contest for freedom, in a remote quarter of the world, could yet find supporters among those who were the most natural and powerful allies of a splendid despotism; that we were the objects of a regard and interest throughout the world, which would add to our own resources sufficient strength to carry us safely through to final success.

★

The Makers of the Flag

by Franklin K. Lane

The work that we do is the making of the Flag.
    I am not the Flag at all, I'm but its shadow.
I'm whatever you make me, nothing more,
    Your dream of what a people may become.
I am song and fear, struggle and panic and ennobling
      hope;
I am the day's work of the weakest man and the
    largest dream of the most daring;
No more than you believe me to be, and all you
    believe I may be—
I am what you make me, nothing more.
I swing before your eyes,
    A bright gleam of color,
A symbol of yourself,
    Suggesting all that makes this nation.
My stars and my stripes,
    Are your dreams and your labors,
They are bright with cheer, brilliant with courage,
    Firm with faith.
Because you have made them so,
    Out of your heart of hearts,
For you are the makers of the Flag
    And 'tis well that you glory in the making!

★

Jefferson's Plan for the Proper Training of Youth

From *The Best Letters of Thomas Jefferson*
Courtesy of Houghton Mifflin Company

From a letter written in Paris, August 19, 1785, by Thomas Jefferson to his nephew, Peter Carr, who grew up in Jefferson's family.

An honest heart being the first blessing, a knowing head is the second. It is time for you now to begin to be choice in your reading; to begin to pursue a regular course in it; and not to suffer [allow] yourself to be turned to the right or left by reading anything out of that course.

I have long ago digested a plan for you, suited to the circumstances in which you will be placed. This I will detail to you, from time to time, as you advance. For the present, I advise you to begin a course of ancient history, reading everything in the original and not in translations.

First read Goldsmith's history of Greece. This will give you a digested view of that field. Then take up ancient history in the detail, reading the following books, in the following order: Herodotus, Thucydides, Xenophontis Anabasis, Arrian, Quintus Curtius, Diodorus Siculus, Justin. This shall form the first stage of your historical reading, and is all I need mention to you now.

The next will be of Roman history. From that, we will come down to modern history. In Greek and Latin poetry, you have read or will read at school, Virgil, Terence, Horace, Anacreon, Theocritus, Homer, Euripides, Sophocles. Read also Milton's *Paradise Lost*, Shakespeare, Ossian, Pope's and Swift's works, in order to form your style in your own language. In morality, read Epictetus, Xenophontis Memorabilia, Plato's Socratic dialogues, Cicero's philosophies, Antoninus, and Seneca.

In order to assure a certain progress in this reading, consider what hours you have free from the school and the exercises of the school. Give about two of them, every day, to exercise; for health must not be sacrificed to learning. A strong body makes the mind strong. As to the species of exercise, I advise the gun. While this gives a moderate exercise to the body, it gives boldness, enterprise, and independence to the mind. Games played with the ball, and others of that nature, are too violent for the body, and stamp no character on the mind. Let your gun, therefore, be the constant companion of your walks. Never think of taking a book with you. The object of walking is to relax the mind.

You should therefore not permit yourself even to think while you walk; but divert yourself by the objects surrounding you.

Walking is the best possible exercise. Habituate yourself to walk very far. The Europeans value themselves on having subdued the horse to the uses of man; but I doubt whether we have not lost more than we have gained, by the use of this animal. Nothing has occasioned so much the degeneracy of the human body. An Indian goes on foot nearly as far in a day, for a long journey, as an enfeebled white does on his horse; and he will tire the best horses. There is no habit you will value so much as that of walking far without fatigue.

I would advise you to take your exercise in the afternoon: not because it is the best time for exercise, for certainly it is not; but because it is the best time to spare from your studies; and habit will soon reconcile it to health, and render it nearly as useful as if you gave to that the more precious hours of the day. A little walk of half an hour, in the morning, when you first rise, is advisable also. It shakes off sleep, and produces other good effects in the animal economy. Rise at a fixed and an early hour, and go to bed at a fixed and early hour also. Sitting up late at night is injurious to the health, and not useful to the mind.

Having ascribed proper hours to exercise, divide what remain (I mean of your vacant hours) into three portions. Give the principal to History, the other two, which should be shorter, to Philosophy and Poetry. Write to me once every month or two, and let me know the progress you make. Tell me in what manner you employ every hour in the day. The plan I have proposed for you is adapted to your present situation only. When that is changed, I shall propose a corresponding change of plan.

I have ordered the following books to be sent to you from London, to the care of Mr. Madison: Herodotus, Thucydides, Xenophon's Hellenics, Anabasis and Memorabilia, Cicero's works, Baretti's Spanish and English Dictionary, Martin's Philosophical Grammar, and Martin's Philosophia Britannica. I will send you the following from here: Bezout's Mathematics, De la Lande's Astronomy, Muschenbrock's Physics, Quintus Curtius, Justin, a Spanish Grammar, and some Spanish books. You will observe that Martin, Bezout, De la Lande, and Muschenbrock, are not in the preceding plan. They are not to be opened till you go to the University. You are now, I expect, learning French. You must push this; because the books which will be put into your hands when you advance into Mathematics, Natural philosophy, Natural history, etc., will be mostly French, these sciences being better treated by the French than the English writers. Our future connection with Spain renders that the most necessary of the modern languages, after the French. When you become a public man, you may have occasion for it, and the circumstances of your possessing that language, may give you a preference over other candidates.

I have nothing further to add for the present, but husband well your time, cherish your instructors, strive to make everybody your friend; and be assured that nothing will be so pleasing as your success to, dear Peter.

"Without Courage, Spirit and Self-Sacrifice No Nation Can Long Exist."
by HENRY CABOT LODGE from *A Fighting Frigate*
From an address delivered in the Old South Church, Boston, October 21, 1897, on the occasion of the return of the frigate Constitution *to the Charlestown Navy Yard*

It is well to note that the lesson of wise preparation, taught by the War of 1812, and always worth remembering, is even more important now than then, for today great wars are fought in a few months, while it takes years to build modern ships and cast rifled guns.

Out of the War of 1812 came these teachings, and out of these teachings, taken to heart, as they were, by the men of that day, came peace, the only peace worth having. One hears it often said, by persons who are prone to mistake for thought the repetition of aged aphorisms, that some people intend to have peace even if they fight for it. They imagine that they are giving utterance to a biting and conclusive sarcasm, when in reality they are stating a profound and simple truth. All the peace the world has ever had has been obtained by fighting, and all the peace that any nation, which is neither subject nor trivial, can ever have, is by readiness to fight if attacked.

In our cities and towns we maintain a large army of soldiers. We call them policemen, but they are drilled and organized, and are in all essentials a military body. For what purpose are they maintained? To make war on any one? On the contrary, we have police in order to keep the public peace. In the same way must the peace of nations be kept.

Weakness, fear, and defenselessness mean war and dishonor. Readiness, preparation, and courage mean honor and peace.

Where we were unprepared in 1812 we suffered; where we were prepared we prospered and vindicated our national existence. That is the true line of national policy for which the *Constitution* stands today just as much as when she overcame the English frigates. Her builder, building better than he knew, both in timber and in words, called her, with a fine eloquence "a powerful agent of national justice." So she was, and she was also a minister and guardian of peace—not the peace at which a spirited people revolts, but the peace of which Lowell sings:

> *Come peace! Not like a mourner bowed,*
> *For honor lost and dear ones wasted,*
> *But proud, to meet a people proud,*
> *With eyes that tell of triumph tasted.*

But there is still something more in this ship *Constitution* than vivid instruction as to the truest national policy. She is the yet living monument, not alone of her own victories, but of the men behind the guns who won them. She speaks to us of patriotism and courage, of the devotion to an idea and to a sentiment for which men laid down their lives.

The distinguished President of a great university has recently warned his students against the tendency "to magnify the savage virtues." It is well recognized that certain virtues can be carried to a point where they cease to be such, but it is not quite clear how a genuine virtue of any kind can be too much magnified. The virtues termed "savage" I take to be the early and primary ones of courage, indifference to danger, and loyalty to the tribes or clans which, in the processes of time, became nations and countries. These primary or "savage" virtues made states and nations possible, and in their very nature are the foundations out of which other virtues have arisen. If they decay, the whole fabric they support will totter and fall.

The gentler virtues, as well as the refinements and graces of civilization, rest upon these simpler qualities, and the highest achievements of the race in the arts of peace have come from the strong, bold nations of the earth. Art, literature, philosophy, invention, in Greece and Rome, in Venice and Holland, all reached their zenith when those countries were at the height of their military and political power, and sank as that power decayed. The discoveries, the education, the freedom, the material development, the vast growth of all which is required to raise and to better the conditions of man-

THE USS CONSTITUTION AND HMS GUERRIERE
By Thomas Birch
In this engagement, which occurred near Cape Race in the War of 1812, the USS Constitution acquired the popular name of "Old Ironsides."

kind, have been most conspicuous and have made the largest progress among those nations which were strongest, most daring, and readiest to defend their rights.

Material success with all that it implies is a great achievement, but it is as nothing to the courage and faith which make men ready to sacrifice all, even their lives, for an ideal or for a sentiment. The men who fell upon the decks of the *Constitution*, or who died at Gettysburg and Shiloh, represent the highest and noblest spirit of which a race is capable. Without that spirit of patriotism, courage, and self-sacrifice no nation can long exist, and the greatest material success in the hands of the cringing and timid will quickly turn to dust and ashes.

Capture of the Guerrière

August 19, 1812 — in the War of 1812

From *The Percy Anecdotes* to which is added a
valuable collection of *American Anecdotes*

The *Constitution* Captain Hull had sailed from Annapolis on the 5th of July. On the 17th, he was chased by a ship of the line and four frigates, when, by an exertion of able sea-manship, than which the victory itself, though more benefi-cial, could not be more worthy of applause, he escaped from the unequal combat.

On the 19th of August, he had an opportunity of trying his frigate against a single vessel of the enemy. This was the *Guerrière*—one of the best of the same class in the British navy, and in no way averse to the rencontre, as she promptly awaited her antagonist's arrival. She had for some time been searching for an American frigate, having given a formal chal-lenge to every vessel of the same description. At one of her mastheads was a flag, on which her name was inscribed in conspicuous letters, and on another, the words, "Not the Little Belt," alluding to the broadsides which the *President* had fired into that sloop before the war.

The *Constitution*, being ready for action, now approached, her crew giving three cheers. Both continued maneuvering for three quarters of an hour. The *Guerrière* attempted to take a raking position, and failing in this, soon afterwards began to pour out her broadsides, with a view of crippling her antagonist. From the *Constitution* not a gun had been fired. Already had an officer twice come on the quarterdeck with information that several of the men had fallen at the guns. Though burning with impatience, the crew silently awaited the orders of their commander.

The long expected moment at length arrived. The vessel being brought exactly to the designed position, directions were given to fire broadside after broadside in quick succes-sion. Never was any scene more dreadful.

For fifteen minutes the lightning of the *Constitution's* guns was a continual blaze, and their thunder roared without inter-mission. The enemy's mizzenmast lay over her side, and she stood exposed to a fire that swept her decks. She became un-manageable; her hull was shattered, her sails and rigging cut to pieces. Her mainmast and foremast fell overboard, taking with them every spar except the bowsprit. The firing then ceased, and the *Guerrière* surrendered. Her loss was fifteen killed and sixty-three wounded; the *Constitution* had seven men killed and seven wounded.

The *Guerrière* was so much damaged as to render it im-possible to bring her into port; she was, therefore, on the following day blown up. The *Constitution* received so little injury that she was in a few hours ready for another action.

Lincoln and the Whetstone

by Edna M. Colman from *Seventy-Five Years of White House Gossip*
Copyright, 1925, by Doubleday, Page & Company

In 1834 when Lincoln was a candidate for the legislature, he called on a certain farmer to ask for his support. He found him in the hay field, and was urging his cause when the dinner bell sounded. The farmer invited him to dinner, but he declined politely, and added, "If you will let me have the scythe while you are gone I will mow round the field a couple of times."

When the farmer returned he found three rows neatly mowed. The scythe lay against the gate post, but Lincoln had disappeared.

Nearly thirty years afterward the farmer and his wife, now grown old, were at a White House reception, and stood waiting in line to shake hands with the President.

When they got near him in the line ... Lincoln saw them, and calling an aide, told him to take them to one of the small parlors, where he would see them as soon as he got through the handshaking. Much surprised, the old couple were led away. Presently Mr. Lincoln came in, and, greeting them with an outstretched hand and a warm smile, called them by name.

"Do you mean to say," exclaimed the farmer, "that you remember me after all these years?"

"I certainly do," said the President, and he went on to recall the day he had mowed around the farmer's timothy field.

"Yes, that's so," said the old man, still in astonishment. "I found the field mowed and the scythe leaning up against the gate post. But I have always wanted to ask you one thing."

"What is it?" asked Mr. Lincoln.

"I always wanted to ask you, Mr. President, what you did with the whetstone?"

Lincoln smoothed his hair back from his brows a moment, in deep thought; then his face lighted up.

"Yes, I remember now," he said, "I put that whetstone on top of the high gate post."

And when he got back to Illinois again, the farmer found the whetstone on top of the gate post, where it had lain for more than twenty-five years.

An Adventure Story as Told in the Indian Symbols

An explanation of the hieroglyphics that stand opposite to
the letters A B C D E F G H I K which are placed at the
side of a column representing the foot of a supposed tree

From *New Voyages to North America* by the Baron Lahontan—1735

If we take the word *hieroglyphic* in its natural sense, 'tis
only a representation of sacred and divine objects, calculated
according to the ideas we have of them. But without any
regard to the etymology, I choose rather to make use of the
common privilege of an infinity of authors in bestowing the
title of hieroglyphic symbols upon all these figures that cor-
respond to the following letters.

A Opposite to this letter you see the arms of France,
with an ax above. Now the ax is a symbol of war among
the savages, as the calumet is the bond of peace: so that this
imports that the French have taken up the ax, or have made
a warlike expedition with as many tens of men as there are
marks or points round the figure. These marks you see are
eighteen in number, and so they signify a hundred and eighty
warriors.

B Over against this letter you meet with a mountain that
represents the city of Montreal (according to the savages),
and the fowl upon the wing at the top signifies departure.
The moon upon the back of the stag signifies the first quarter
of the July moon, which is called the stag-moon.

C Opposite to this letter you detect a canoe, signifying
that they have traveled by water as many days as you see
huts in the figure; that is, twenty-one days.

D Upon the same parallel with this letter, you see a foot,
meaning that after their voyage by water, they marched on
foot as many days as there are huts designed; that is, for
seven days, each day's journey for the warriors being as much
as five common French leagues, or five of those which are
reckoned to be twenty in a degree.

E By this letter you perceive a hand and three huts,
which signify that they are within a three-day journey of
the Iroquois Tsonnontouans, whose arms are a hut with two
trees leaning downwards, as you see them drawn. The sun
imports that they were just to the eastward of the village,

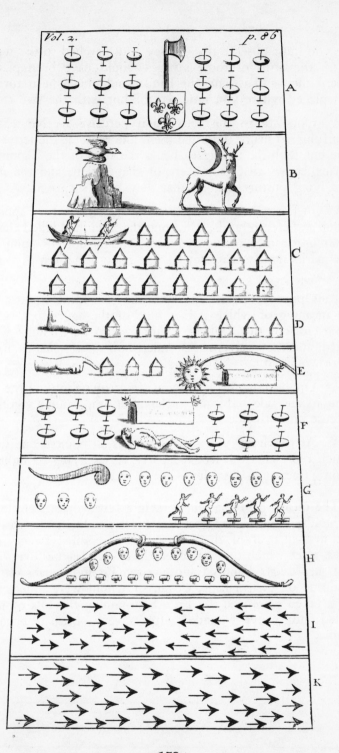

for you must observe that if they had marched to the westward, the arms of those savages would have been placed where the hand is, and the hand would have been turned and placed where you now see the hut with the two trees.

F Opposite to this letter you perceive twelve marks, signifying so many times ten men, like those at the letter A. The hut with the two trees, being the arms of the Tsonnontouans, shows that they were of that nation; and the man in a lying posture denotes that they were surprised.

G In the row which answers to this letter, there appears a club and eleven heads, indicating that they had killed eleven Tsonnontouans, and the five men standing upright upon the five marks signify that they took as many times ten prisoners of war.

H Opposite to this letter you see nine heads in an arch, the meaning of which is that nine of the aggressors, or of the victorious side (which I supposed to be French) were killed; and the twelve marks underneath signify that as many were wounded.

I Opposite to this letter you see arrows flying in the air, some to one side and some to the other, importing a vigorous defense on both sides.

K At this letter you see the arrows all pointed one way, which represents the worsted party either flying or fighting upon a retreat in disorder.

The meaning of the whole is, in a few words, as follows. A hundred and eighty Frenchmen set out from Montreal in the first quarter of the July moon and sailed twenty-one days, after which they marched thirty-five leagues over land and surprised a hundred and twenty Tsonnontouans on the east side of their village, eleven of whom were killed, and fifty taken prisoners, the French sustaining the loss of nine killed and twelve wounded, after a very obstinate engagement.

Travel Adventures in the Colony of Georgia about 1790

From *Travels through North and South Carolina, Georgia, East and West Florida, the Cherokee Country, the Extensive Territories of the Muscogulges or Creek Confederacy, and the Country of the Choctaws*

by WILLIAM BARTRAM — 1791

Now I am come within the atmosphere of the illicium groves, how reanimating is the fragrance! Every part of this plant above ground possesses an aromatic scent, but the large pericarp is the most fragrant of it, which continually perspires an oleaginous sweat, as warm and stimulating as cloves or mace. I never saw it grow naturally farther north than Lat. 33°, on the Mobile River and its branches, and only one place in East Florida near Lake George, Lat. 28°.

About the middle of the afternoon we were joyfully surprised at the distant prospect of the trading company coming up, and we soon met, saluting each other several times with a general Indian whoop, or shout of friendship; then each company came to camp within a few paces of each other, and before night I struck up a bargain with them for a handsome, strong young horse, which cost me about ten pounds sterling. I was now forced to leave my old horse behind, to feed in rich cane pastures, where he was to remain and renew his spirits until the return of his new master from Mobile, from whom I extorted a promise to use him gently and, if possible, not to make a pack horse of him.

Next morning we decamped, proceeding again on our travels, now alert and cheerful, crossed a brisk rivulet rippling over a gravelly bed, and winding through aromatic groves of the Illicium Floridanum, then gently descended to the high forests, leaving Deadman's Creek, for at this creek a white man was found dead, supposed to have been murdered, from which circumstance it has its name.

A few days before we arrived in Indian territory, we met a company of emigrants from Georgia—a man, his wife, a young woman, several young children, and three stout young men, with about a dozen horses loaded with their property. They informed us their design was to settle on the Alabama, a few miles above its confluence with the Tombigbe.

Being now near Indian territory, the chief trader with another of our company set off ahead to give notice to the tribe of his approach with the merchandise, each of them taking the best horse he could pick out of the gang, leaving the goods to the conduct and care of a young Indian and myself.

Early in the evening we came to the banks of a large, deep creek—a considerable branch of the Alabama. The waters ran furiously, being overcharged with the floods of rain which had fallen the day before. We discovered immediately that there was no possibility of crossing it by fording. Its depth and rapidity would have swept our horses, loads and all, instantly from our sight.

My companion, after consideration, said we must make a raft to ferry over our goods, which we immediately set about, after unloading our horses and turning them out to range. I undertook to collect dry canes, and my companion, dry timber or logs and vines to bind them together. Having gathered the necessary materials and laid them in order on the banks of the river, ready to work upon, we betook ourselves to repose, and early next morning set about building our raft.

This was a novel scene to me, and I could not, until the raft was finished and put to practice, well comprehend how it could possibly answer the effect desired. In the first place we laid, parallel to each other, dry, sound trunks of trees, about nine feet in length and eight or nine inches in diameter, binding them fast together with grapevines and tough, flexible branches until we had formed the main deck, about twelve or fourteen feet in length. We then bound the dry canes in bundles, each nearly as thick as a man's body, with which we formed the sides, laying them close to each other and binding them fast. After this manner our raft was constructed.

Then having two strong grapevines, each long enough to cross the river, we fastened one to each end of the raft, which was now completed, and loaded on as much as it would safely carry. The Indian took the end of one of the vines in his mouth, plunged into the river, and swam over with it, and the vine attached to the other end was committed to my charge, to steady the raft and haul it back again after being unloaded. As soon as he had safely landed and hauled taut his vine, I pushed off the raft, which he drew over as quickly as possible, I steadying it with my vine. In this manner, though with inexpressible danger of losing our effects, we ferried everything safely over.

The last load contained my property, with all my clothes, which I had stripped off except for my breeches, for they contained matters of more value and consequence than all the rest of my property put together; besides, I did not choose to expose myself entirely naked to the alligators and serpents in crossing the flood.

Now seeing all the goods safely over and the horses at a landing place on the banks of the river about fifty yards above, I drove them all in together, and seeing them safely landed, I plunged in after them, and being a tolerable swimmer, soon reached the opposite shore. But my difficulties were not yet at an end, for our horses all landed just below the mouth of a considerable branch of this river, of fifteen or twenty feet in width, with perpendicular banks almost as many feet in height above its swift waters, over which we were obliged to carry every article of our effects—by no other bridge than a sapling felled across it, which is called a raccoon bridge. Over this my Indian friend would trip as quick and light as that quadruped, with one hundred-weight of leather on his back, when I was scarcely able to shuffle myself along over it astride.

At last having repacked and set off again, without any material occurrence intervening, in the evening we arrived at the banks of the great Tallapoose River and came to camp under shelter of some Indian cabins in expansive fields close to the river bank, opposite the town of Savannah. Late in the evening a young white man, in great haste and seeming confusion, joined our camp and immediately related that while on his journey from Pensacola, it happened that the very night after we had passed the company of emigrants, he met them and joined their camp in the evening. Just at dark, the Choctaws surrounded them, plundered their camp, and carried all the people off captive except himself, he having the good fortune to escape with his horse, though closely pursued.

Next morning very early, though very cold, and the surface of the earth as hoary as if covered with a fall of snow, the trader, standing on the opposite shore entirely naked except for a breechcloth, and encircled by a company of red men in similar apparel, hailed us, and presently, with canoes, brought us all over with the merchandise and conducted us safely to a nearby town.

The next day was a day of rest and audience; the following

was devoted to feasting, and the evening concluded in celebrating the nuptials of the young Indian with a Creek girl—daughter of the chief and sister of our trader's wife. The trader's house and stores formed a complete square, after the mode of the habitations of the Muscogulges; that is, four oblong buildings of equal dimensions, two opposite to each other, encompassing an area of about a quarter of an acre. On one side of this a fence enclosed a yard of nearly an acre of ground, at one of the far corners of which a booth or pavilion was formed of green boughs, with two laurel trees planted in front. This was the secret nuptial chamber. Dancing, music, and feasting continued the first part of the night, and towards morning the happy couple privately withdrew, and continued alone all the next day, no one presuming to approach the sacred, mysterious bridal chamber.

The trader obliged me with his company on a visit to the Alabama, an Indian town at the confluence of the two fine rivers, the Tallapoose and Coosau, which here resign their names to the great Alabama, where are to be seen traces of the ancient French fortress, Toulouse. Here are still lying, half buried in the earth, a few pieces of weapons, including four and six pounders. I observed two or three very large apple trees in a very thriving condition, planted here by the French.

This is, perhaps, one of the most ideal locations for a city in the world—a level plain between the conflux of two majestic rivers which are exactly of equal magnitude in appearance, each navigable for vessels and large canoes at least five hundred miles above it, and spreading their numerous branches over the most fertile and delightful regions, many hundred miles before we reach their sources in the Appalachian mountains.

⁓⁓⁓

Whoe'er has travell'd life's dull round,
  Where'er his stages may have been,
May sigh to think he still has found
  The warmest welcome at an inn.

—*William Shenstone*
Written on a window of an inn

"Most Americans Do Not Know the Constitution"

A Historic Television Interview with Justice Hugo L. Black

by BILL IRVIN
Reprinted, courtesy of *Chicago Today*, successor to *Chicago's American*

Hugo L. Black, senior justice of the Supreme Court, believes the court's 1954 landmark decision ordering desegregation throughout the country has delayed the progress of desegregation.

Justice Black also says the court was merely following the Constitution in handing down decisions which have been widely blamed for making law enforcement more difficult.

The 82-year-old justice also believes the word "obscenity" is wholly ambiguous and says he always has detested it.

These were a few of the wide range of topics Black touched on in an unprecedented hour television interview last night on CBS, "Justice Black and the Bill of Rights."

Conducting the questioning in the study of Justice Black's home in Alexandria, Virginia, were CBS correspondents Martin Agronsky and Eric Sevareid.

"As far as we know," said Sevareid, "there is no precedent for a television interview with a sitting judge, who talks about the law, the Constitution, and the court."

Black's appointment to the court in 1937 by President Franklin D. Roosevelt created a furor when it became known that the then Senator Black had been a member of the Ku Klux Klan for a short time as a young politician in his home state of Alabama.

In his thirty-one years on the high court, twenty-three of them as senior justice, more of Justice Black's dissents "have later become the majority opinion and the law of the land than is true of any other Supreme Court justice ever," Sevareid noted.

Frequently during the interview, Justice Black referred to a small, well-thumbed copy of the Constitution which he said he always carries with him.

"I don't know the Constitution by heart," he said, "and when I quote from it I want to be accurate."

Justice Black said most Americans don't know the Constitution. They all think it prohibits the things they think should be prohibited and approves things they think should be approved.

"Some people have said I'm either a knave or a fool," said the justice good-humoredly. "I get letters telling me to go back to Russia. That's too far to go because I've never been there."

On the court's 1954 desegregation decision, Justice Black said:

"Looking back at it now, it seems to have delayed the process of desegregation. I believe that case [Brown vs. School Board] should have been treated as an ordinary lawsuit not applicable only to the counties involved. That would have fitted into my philosophy of not making decisions to apply to the entire nation."

Agronsky asked if being assigned to write the majority opinion in a case would affect his decision. Black said:

"My vote is mine. I'll vote it my way."

Sevareid asked why there has been so much civil disorder in the country.

"This country has always been known as a country of violence," said Black. "George Washington had to send the army to put down the whisky rebellion in Pennsylvania."

"Did court decisions hamper the police in law enforcement?" asked Sevareid. "The court didn't do it," said the justice. "That's a little off. It was the Constitution. It guarantees an accused person the right to a lawyer, protects people against unreasonable search and seizure."

Black was asked about the disorders during the Democratic convention in Chicago.

He said he didn't want to express an opinion about them because a case growing out of the convention-week violence is pending before the court.

The justice pointed out that one side claims the protesters were idealistic.

"No group has the Constitutional right to use other people's property for protesting," said the justice.

"The Constitution doesn't say that any man shall have a right to say anything he wishes anywhere he wants to go. It does not say people shall have a right to assemble to express views on other people's property."

He said he knows of nothing that "gives people the right to tramp up and down the streets by the thousands."

Asked about how he felt about Franklin D. Roosevelt, Black said he considered him a "great" man.

He said he never heard from Roosevelt about how he should vote on cases pending before the court.

As for President Truman, "I always liked Harry," said the justice.

"After I heard him make a campaign speech," said Black, "I called him and said if he spoke that way during his campaign, he could be elected. Harry agreed with me. They should never have written that man off."

Sevareid asked who in modern times could measure up to the requirements for the high court among those not having a legal background. Justice Black answered:

"Walter Lippmann."

"We have the best Constitution in the world," said Justice Black, "and if we follow it, we'll be all right."

December 4, 1968

Constitutions should consist only of general provisions; the reason is that they must necessarily be permanent, and that they cannot calculate for the possible change of things.

—*Alexander Hamilton*

I consider the foundation of the Constitution as laid on this ground—that all powers not delegated to the United States, by the Constitution, nor prohibited by it to the states, are reserved to the states, or to the people. To take a single step beyond . . . is to take possession of a boundless field of power.

—*Thomas Jefferson*

The basis of our political systems is the right of the people to make and to alter their constitutions of government. But the constitution which at any time exists, until changed by an explicit and authentic act of the whole people, is sacredly obligatory upon all. —*George Washington*

*

Basic Qualities of Dwight Eisenhower:
Modesty and Civilian Touch

by JOHN GUNTHER from *Procession*

One of Eisenhower's principal sources of power is his obvious integrity, his sincerity and capacity to inspire confidence. Years ago I met a British general in Algiers who had just had his first contact with him as commander in chief. His words were, "By Jove, what a person to rely on!" The General's liking for people, his spontaneity, his instinctive ability to understand the other person's point of view, make him little short of a prodigy at personal relationships, though he sometimes seems to lack humor. And his charm is legendary. When he enters a room, almost any room, a ripple of emotion seizes those present; they catch his glow.

Another quality is his directness. Nothing in his whole life so revolted him as his first glimpse of a Nazi "horror camp"—the concentration camp at Ohrdruf, near Gotha, which he saw just after its liberation by American forces, before the piles of bones could be hidden or the last of the starving, miserable, incredibly emaciated prisoners done to death. Within an hour, he dispatched a message to the Secretary of War in Washington asking that a delegation of American publicists and politicians be flown to Europe at once so that they could see these unbelievable horrors firsthand, before the camp was cleaned up. Then—an acute Eisenhower idea – he forced German *civilians* (not soldiers, who might be expected to be in tune with such savagery) in the nearby towns to bury the dead. The mayor of one such town, who had never known that such things existed in his neighborhood, committed suicide with his wife that night. Eisenhower, when he heard this, exclaimed "Good!" He was delighted to find that some Germans at least had a sense of shame and "a few sensibilities left."

Eisenhower is indisputably one of the most modest men who ever attained a great station, but this does not mean that he is not sure of himself. One of his most valuable qualities—practicality—arises out of this assurance. But the humility is genuine; the modesty is not mock. He said to a friend once, "My only satisfaction in life is to hope that my effort means something to the other fellow. What can I do to repay society for the wonderful opportunities it has given me?" In the great Guildhall speech in London in June, 1945, he said, "Humility must always be the portion of any man who receives acclaim earned in the blood of his followers and the sacrifices of his friends."

In strict contradistinction to some other commanders, he never permitted correspondents during the war to dateline their stories "General Eisenhower's Headquarters." The term had to be "Allied Headquarters."

One story, which members of his staff today neither confirm nor deny, is that, when offered the Congressional Medal of Honor by Mr. Roosevelt, he turned it down. He had done nothing in the realm of personal heroism to deserve it, he insisted. If this legend is correct, Eisenhower is certainly the only man in American history ever to have refused this supreme decoration. Of course for a man to have no vanity at all would be the greatest of all vanities. Therefore it is a pleasure to report that Eisenhower did, once or twice, behave quite normally and register his delight at an accomplishment, or confess to a legitimate ambition. For some days in November, 1942, he was in operational command of the fortress of Gibraltar; this excited him so much that he scribbled a memorandum about it longhand. His permanent rank at that time was, incredibly enough, only lieutenant colonel; yet he was bossing British field marshals, and he could not help being amazed at his own position. On another occasion he confessed that he had always hoped that he would be promoted to the grade of four-star general, if he ever reached this grade, on the actual field of battle.

Finally we come back to the essential master point that Eisenhower is so civilian-minded. In fact, though he has spent his whole life as a soldier, he actually seems to *be* a civilian; he wears civilian clothes quite often, and even likes to make cracks about "the Pentagon mind." One of my French friends, meeting him for the first time, burst out recently with the words "But he is such a nonmilitary general!" Plenty of Europeans think that some crazy American officer may drop one of our atomic bombs for fun someday. They know that Eisenhower won't.

His speeches are to a remarkable extent packed with antiwar sentiment. He harps again and again on the fact that our generation has been twice defaced by war, and that war must not come again. He talks about the "crime" and "waste" of war and its "beastliness." He said on one occasion, "I hate war as only a soldier who has lived it can, only as one who has seen its brutality, its futility, its *stupidity*." He talks of the "dark ground of prejudice, fear, hysteria—the soil in which the evil seeds of war flourish." On another occasion he told a graduating class (of civilians), "Your business is to put me out of business."

Here are some further Eisenhower sentiments on the subject:

> Total war would be the suicide of our generation.
> We must train the youth of America to avert World War III, not to refight World War II.
> Belligerence is the hallmark of insecurity.
> There is no glory in battle worth the blood it costs.

His prestige, which was great anyway, has as a result of all this become greater, particularly in Europe. He has become the first citizen of Europe. Many on the continent grab his words as if they were meat, bread, and guns, because he is the general who is going to *prevent* a war, not make one. Europe's prevailing mood these days is to hope for peace; and Eisenhower, though he would be the first to resist attack, is an eloquent symbol of this mood. He gives people confidence that he really *believes* in peace; more than this, and above all, that peace is a reasonable objective that he is strong enough to attain.

Field Marshal Lord Montgomery is supposed to have made a little joke recently: "If Ike returns to the United States to run for President, I'll have to go there too and campaign against him, in order to keep him here."

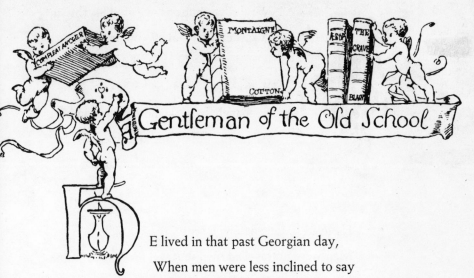

A Gentleman of the Old School

HE lived in that past Georgian day,
    When men were less inclined to say
That "Time is Gold," and overlay
       With toil their pleasure;
He held some land, and dwelt thereon,—
Where, I forget,—the house is gone;
His Christian name, I think, was John,—
       His surname, Leisure.

Reynolds has painted him,—a face
Filled with a fine, old-fashioned grace,
Fresh-colored, frank, with ne'er a trace
       Of trouble shaded;
The eyes are blue, the hair is drest
In plainest way,—one hand is prest
Deep in a flapped canary vest,
       With buds brocaded.

He wears a brown old Brunswick coat,
With silver buttons,—round his throat,
A soft cravat;—in all you note
    An elder fashion,—
A strangeness, which, to us who shine
In shapely hats,—whose coats combine
All harmonies of hue and line,
    Inspires compassion.

He lived so long ago, you see!
Men were untravelled then, but we,
Like Ariel, post o'er land and sea
    With careless parting;
He found it quite enough for him
To smoke his pipe in "garden trim,"
And watch, about the fish tank's brim,
    The swallows darting.

He liked the well-wheel's creaking tongue,—
He liked the thrush that stopped and sung,—
He liked the drone of flies among
      His netted peaches;
He liked to watch the sunlight fall
Athwart his ivied orchard wall;
Or pause to catch the cuckoo's call
      Beyond the beeches.

His were the times of Paint and Patch,
And yet no Ranelagh could match
The sober doves that round his thatch
      Spread tails and sidled;
He liked their ruffling, puffed content,—
For him their drowsy wheelings meant
More than a Mall of Beaux that bent,
      Or Belles that bridled.

Not that, in truth, when life began
He shunned the flutter of the fan;
He too had maybe "pinked his man"
      In Beauty's quarrel;
But now his "fervent youth" had flown
Where lost things go; and he was grown
As staid and slow-paced as his own
      Old hunter, Sorrel.

Yet still he loved the chase, and held

That no composer's score excelled

The merry horn, when Sweetlip swelled

   Its jovial riot;

But most his measured words of praise

Caressed the angler's easy ways,—

His idly meditative days,—

   His rustic diet.

Not that his "meditating" rose

Beyond a sunny summer doze;

He never troubled his repose

   With fruitless prying;

But held, as law for high and low,

What God withholds no man can know,

And smiled away inquiry so,

   Without replying.

We read—alas, how much we read!—
The jumbled strifes of creed and creed
With endless controversies feed
  Our groaning tables;
His books—and they sufficed him—were
Cotton's "Montaigne," The Grave" of Blair,
A "Walton"—much the worse for wear,
  And "Æsop's Fables."

One more,—"The Bible." Not that he
Had searched its page as deep as we;
No sophistries could make him see
  Its slender credit;
It may be that he could not count
The sires and sons of Jesse's fount,—
He liked the "Sermon on the Mount,"—
  And more, he read it.

Once he had loved, but failed to wed,
A red-cheeked lass who long was dead;
His ways were far too slow, he said,
  To quite forget her;
And still when time had turned him gray,
The earliest hawthorn buds in May
Would find his lingering feet astray,
  Where first he met her.

"*In Cœlo Quies*" heads the stone

On Leisure's grave,—now little known,

A tangle of wild-rose has grown

    So thick across it;

Sorrel

The "Benefactions" still declare

He left the clerk an elbow-chair,

And "12 Pence Yearly to Prepare

    A Christmas Posset."

Lie softly, Leisure! Doubtless you,

    With too serene a conscience drew

Your easy breath, and slumbered through

    The gravest issue;

But we, to whom our age allows

Scarce space to wipe our weary brows,

Look down upon your narrow house,

    Old friend, and miss you!

Especially
for
the Ladies

Why a Boat Is a "She"

From *The Bangor Daily News*

A boat is called a "she" because
    —there's always a great deal of bustle about her.
    —there's usually a gang of men around her.
    —she has a waist and stays.
    —it takes a lot of paint to keep her looking good.
    —it's not the initial expense that breaks you, it's the upkeep.
    —she's all decked out.
    —it takes a good man to handle her right.
    —she shows her topsides, hides her bottom, and
        when coming into port always heads for the buoys.

❖❖❖❖❖

A Game of Fives

From *Phantasmagoria* by LEWIS CARROLL

Five little girls of Five, Four, Three, Two, One:
Rolling on the hearthrug, full of tricks and fun.

Five rosy girls, in years from Ten to Six:
Sitting down to lessons—no more time for tricks.

Five growing girls, from Fifteen to Eleven:
Music, Drawing, Languages, and food enough for seven!

Five winsome girls, from Twenty to Sixteen:
Each young man that calls, I say "Now tell me which
    you *mean!*"

Five dashing girls, the youngest Twenty-one:
But, if nobody proposes, what is there to be done?

Five showy girls—but Thirty is an age
When girls may be *engaging,* but they somehow don't
    engage.

Five dressy girls, of Thirty-one or more:
So gracious to the shy young men they snubbed so much
    before!

Salad

To make this condiment, your poet begs
The pounded yellow of two hard-boiled eggs;
Two boiled potatoes, passed through kitchen sieve,
Smoothness and softness to the salad give.
Let onion atoms lurk within the bowl,
And, half suspected, animate the whole.

Of mordant mustard add a single spoon;
Distrust the condiment that bites so soon;
But deem it not, thou man of herbs, a fault
To add a double quantity of salt.
And lastly o'er the flavored compound toss
A magic soup spoon of anchovy sauce.

Oh, green and glorious! Oh, herbaceous treat!
'Twould tempt the dying anchorite to eat;
Back to the world he'd turn his fleeting soul,
And plunge his fingers in the salad bowl;
Serenely full, the epicure would say,
"Fate cannot harm me, I have dined today!"

It's the Custom

by Howard Vincent O'Brien from *All Things Considered*
Copyright, 1948, by The Bobbs-Merrill Company

My role in the wedding is small. I have fewer lines than the doorman. All I say is, "I do" (or do I?) as I hand the bride over to the church and the young man who may be able to manage her better than I have ever been able to do. From then on I play no part in the business.

Despite the negligible importance of my act, I am being rehearsed in it as if I were to deliver the soliloquy from *Hamlet*. Not only am I coached as to gait, stance and follow-through, but my costume is the subject of as much debate as if I were a debutante being presented at the Court of St. James's.

It all takes me back to the days—or day, to be precise—when I was on the stage. Yes, I'm an old-timer in show business. I played with Mansfield. I still remember the rich color of the master's language when he ordered me to get down—and I got down on my hands and knees, not knowing that "down," in the jargon of the theater, means the front of the stage.

All the honors were not Mansfield's, however. In the big scene of the play I was one of several who carried spears and stood guarding the various exits. Came the moment when Mansfield shouted, "Away! Away!" or something like that and was supposed to disappear through one of these exits. Before he could do it, the guard (an accomplice of mine) blocked the way with his spear. Mansfield, a quick-witted fellow, turned to another exit, but the guard at that one also dropped his spear. Mansfield realized then that he was cornered and made an ignominious way out through the wings. Almost immediately thereafter several spear carriers were "at liberty," as we say in the profession.

Coming back to weddings, I must say that I am puzzled by the attention lavished on my part in the one which is soon to take place at our house. As far as anyone would notice, I might appear in dungarees or diapers. This may seem an excessive statement, but a friend of mine once went to a party fully dressed above the waist, but in flannel smallclothes below—and it was twenty minutes before anybody noticed anything wrong with the picture.

The ether vibrates these days with voices pleading for laws for or against something, as if laws ever accomplished anything for good or ill. The fact of the matter is that the human race is governed by convention far more than it is by law. Take, for example, that perfect sample of convention—the wedding invitation. There is no law, human or divine, which requires that it be engraved. And certainly there is nothing handed down from the Medes and the Persians which speci-fies the spare envelope inside the outside, or traveling, envelope. If the human mind really delighted in efficiency, as it is supposed to; if it really preferred the straight line between points, as we are taught in the textbooks, a printed post card would suffice to acquaint people with the fact that they were wanted at a wedding.

But the human mind does *not* delight in being practical. It delights in waste motion. It would rather travel round about than straight ahead. That is why we have such things as political conventions and never miss an opportunity to thumb our noses at logic. Pretending to be reasonable creatures, we stumble along under the weight of yester-day's ten thousand years. What was good enough for our ancestors is good enough for us, and there is nothing for which we have so little taste as progress. Even when we are forced to drop engraving for speedier and more efficient ways of transmitting the written word, we insist on a letter which imitates copperplate. We are, in short, creatures of habit.

That is why the French, wise in the ways of men, explain away every absurdity of life with a shrug of the shoulders and the simple yet profound phrase: "It's the custom."

Young and Old

From *The Water Babies* by CHARLES KINGSLEY

When all the world is young, lad,
    And all the trees are green;
And every goose a swan, lad,
    And every lass a queen;
Then hey for boot and horse, lad,
    And round the world away;
Young blood must have its course, lad,
    And every dog his day.

When all the world is old, lad,
    And all the trees are brown;
And all the sport is stale, lad,
    And all the wheels run down;
Creep home, and take your place there,
    The spent and maimed among:
God grant you find one face there,
    You loved when all was young.

The Complaint of the Convalescent

by GERALDINE MEYRICK

When you're sick in bed of something
  And hate the sight of food;
When the tinkle of a teaspoon
  Is torture to your mood;
Nurse will come to you at intervals
  That haven't any length
And it's: "Eat this all, now, quickly,
  For you must keep up your strength."

But when you're really better
   And your appetite is fine;
When your chief and only longing
   Is substantially to dine;
Nurse will bring you something sloppy
   After ages, ages, long;
And it's: "Just a little, slowly,
   For you know you are not strong!"

Oh, it may be she's an angel —
   I have thought she was, myself —
But now I am so hungry—
   Is there nothing on the shelf?
I want some cheese and crackers
   Or a slice of cold mince pie;
And it's: "You may have some jelly,
   Lemon jelly, bye and bye."

Children

by Henry Wadsworth Longfellow

Come to me, O ye children!
   For I hear you at your play;
And the questions that perplexed me
   Have vanished quite away.

Ye open the Eastern windows,
   That look towards the sun,
Where thoughts are singing swallows,
   And the brooks of morning run.

For what are all our contrivings
   And the wisdom of our books,
When compared with your caresses,
   And the gladness of your looks!

Ye are better than all the ballads
   That ever were sung or said;
For ye are living poems,
   And all the rest are dead.

Snared in Her Own Trap

From *Ten Years among the Mail Bags* by J. HOLBROOK, a post office inspector

A lady of a very genteel and respectable appearance, called one day on a prominent New England postmaster, with a letter in her hand, which she insisted had been broken open and resealed. She handed the letter to the postmaster, who examined it, and appearances certainly seemed to justify her assertion. She further declared that she well knew which clerk in the office had broken it open, and that he had previously served several of her letters in the same way. Upon hearing this, the postmaster requested her to walk inside the office, and point out the person whom she suspected.

Such an unusual phenomenon as the appearance of a lady inside the office produced, as may be supposed, a decided sensation among the clerks there assembled. Nor was the sensation diminished in intensity when the postmaster informed them that the lady was there for the purpose of identifying the person who had been guilty of breaking open her letters!

This announcement at once excited the liveliest feelings of curiosity and solicitude in the mind of almost everyone present, and each one, conscious of innocence, indulged in conjectures as to who that somebody else might be, whom the accusing Angel(?) was to fix upon as the culprit.

All their conjectures fell wide of the mark. After looking about for a moment, the lady pointed out the last man whom anyone in the office would have suspected of such an offense— one of the oldest and most reliable of their number.

"That is the person," said she, indicating him by a slight nod of the head; "and if he persists in making so free with my letters, I will certainly have him arrested. Why my letters should always be selected for this purpose, I cannot imagine; but if any more of them are touched, he will wish he had let them alone."

This direct charge, and these threats, produced a greater commotion among his fellow clerks, than in the mind of the gentleman accused. Waiting for a moment after she had spoken, he broke the breathless silence that followed her words, by saying calmly, —"Mrs. ———, I believe?"

"That is my name, sir."

"Have you concluded your remarks, madam?"

"I have, sir, for the present."

"Then, madam, I will take the liberty to inform you that *your husband* is the person on whom you ought to expend your indignation. He has, at different times, taken several of your letters from the office, opened and read them, and after resealing, returned them to the letter box, having made certain discoveries in those letters, to which he forced me to listen, as furnishing sufficient ground for his course, and justifying former suspicions! He earnestly requested me never to disclose who had opened the letters, and I should have continued to observe secrecy, had not your accusation forced me to this disclosure in self-defense. If you wish to have my statement corroborated, I think I can produce a reliable witness."

The lady did not reply to this proposition, but made a precipitate retreat, leaving the clerk master of the field, and was never afterwards seen at that post office.

Mother to Son

From *Selected Poems* by LANGSTON HUGHES

Well, son, I'll tell you:
Life for me ain't been no crystal stair,
It's had tracks in it,
And splinters,
And boards torn up
And places with no carpet on the floor—
Bare.
But all the time
I'se been a-climbin' on,
And reachin' landin's
And turnin' corners,
And sometimes goin' in the dark
Where there ain't been no light,
So, boy, don't you turn back,
Don't you set down on the steps
'Cause you find it kinder hard;
Don't you fall now—
For I'se still goin', honey.
I'se still climbin',
And life for me ain't been no crystal stair.

The Three Wishes

by Edmund Vance Cooke

"Well, now," drawled the fairy, "I'll give you three wishes."
"Not me," said the housewife, "I'm not superstitious;
Yet I think you'd be put in a bit of a box,
If I wished that my husband wore self-darning socks."

" 'Tis done," said the fairy, "this day they begin
If ever they ravel to heal like his skin."
"Well, then," said the housewife, "as wishes are reckoned,
I figure my next wish is only my second,
And so, to escape a detestable chore,
I wish every room had a self-sweeping floor."

The fairy's face darkened. "You're very adept
At wishing," she cried, "but your floors shall be swept,
And if too cleanly swept, recollect you preferred
To trifle with fortune. And now for the third."

"Oh, well," said the housewife, "the last of my wishes
Is simple enough. I want self-washing dishes!"
The good fairy screamed and went up in the air;
"I shall picket your house! I shall post you 'Unfair'!

Had you asked me for rubies or royal connection,
For moderate hips or a paint-proof complexion,
For fame in the movies, or freedom from bunions,
For a violet breath, after suppers of onions,
But to ask me—a fairy, a miniature mystic,
For self-washing dishes—the thing's—Bolshevistic!"

The Romance of the Frontier

by WILLIAM W. FOWLER from *Woman on the American Frontier—1876*

The young married people, who form a considerable part of the pioneer element in our country, are simple in their habits, moderate in their aspirations, and hoard a little old-fashioned romance—unconsciously enough—in the secret nooks of their rustic hearts. They find no fault with their bare loggeries; with a shelter and a handful of furniture, they have enough. If there is the wherewithal to spread a warm supper for the "old man" when he comes in from work, the young wife forgets the long, solitary, wordless day and asks no greater happiness than preparing it by the help of such materials and utensils as would be looked at with utter contempt in the comfortable kitchens of the East.

They have youth, hope, health, occupation, and amusement, and when you have added "meat, clothes, and fire," what more has England's queen?

We should, however, remember that there is another large class of women who, for various reasons, have left comfortable homes in older communities, and risked their happiness and all that they have in enterprises of pioneer life in the far West. What wonder that they should sadly miss the thousand old familiar means and appliances! Some utensil or implement necessary to their husbandry is wanting or has been lost or broken, and cannot be replaced. Some comfort or luxury to which she has been used from childhood is lacking, and cannot be furnished. The multifarious materials upon which household art can employ itself are reduced to the few absolute essentials. These difficulties are felt more by the woman than the man. To quote the words of a writer who was herself a pioneer housewife in the West:

"The husband goes to his work with the same axe or hoe which fitted his hand in his old woods and fields; he tills the same soil or perhaps a far richer and more hopeful one; he gazes on the same book of nature which he has read from his infancy and sees only a fresher and more glowing page, and he returns home with the sun, strong in heart and full of self congratulation on the favorable change in his lot. Perhaps he finds the home bird drooping and disconsolate. She has found a thousand difficulties which her rougher mate can scarcely be taught to feel as evils. She has been looking in vain for any of the cherished features of her old fireside. What cares he if the time-honored cupboard is meagerly represented by a few oak boards lying on pegs called shelves. His tea equipage shines as always, the biscuits can hardly stay on the brightly glistening plates. His bread never was better baked. What does he want with the great old-fashioned rocking chair? When he is tired he goes to bed, for he is never tired till bedtime. The sacrifices in moving West have been made most largely by women."

It is this very dearth of so many things that once made her life easy and comfortable which throws her back upon her own resources. Here again is woman's strength. Fertile in expedients, apt in device, an artisan to construct and an artist to embellish, she proceeds to supply what is lacking in her new home. She has a miraculous faculty for creating much out of little, and for transforming the coarse into the beautiful. Barrels are converted into easy chairs and washstands; spring beds are manufactured with rows of slender, elastic saplings; a box covered with muslin stuffed with hay serves for a lounge. By the aid of considerable personal exertion, while she adds to the list of useful and necessary articles, she also enlarges the circle of luxuries. An hour or two of extra work now and then enables her to hoard enough to buy a new looking glass, and to make from time to time small additions to the showy part of the household.

After she has transformed the rude cabin into a cozy habitation, she turns her attention to the outside surroundings. Woodbine and wild cucumber are trailed over the doors and windows; little beds of sweet williams and marigolds line the path to the clearing's edge or across the prairie to the well; and an apple or pear tree is put in here and there. In all these works, either of use or embellishment, if not done by her own hand, she is at least the moving spirit.

A Farewell

by CHARLES KINGSLEY

My fairest child, I have no song to give you;
  No lark could pipe to skies so dull and gray;
Yet, ere we part, one lesson I can leave you
  For every day.

Be good, sweet maid, and let who will be clever;
  Do noble things, not dream them, all day long:
And so make life, death, and that vast forever
  One grand, sweet song.

Life

by Anne Campbell

A little house to keep,
A little floor to sweep.
A little meal to make,
A little sweet to bake.
A little friend to know,
A little flower to grow.
A little bird to sing,
A little hand to cling.
A little child's caress,
A little life to bless.
A little grief and pain,
A little cheer again.
A little fleeting day,
A little prayer to say.
A little house to keep,
There is no joy so deep.

In Truth, Women's Work Was Never Done!

From *The Every-Day Book, 1826*—An Almanac by WILLIAM HONE

Now come the long evenings with devices for amusing them. In the intervals of recreation there is "work to do." This word "work" is significant of an employment which astonishes men, and seems never to tire the fingers of their industrious helpmates and daughters; except that, with an expression which we are at a loss to take for either jest or earnest, because it partakes of each, they now and then exclaim, "women's work is never done!"

The assertion is not exactly the fact, but it is not a great way from it. What "man of woman born" ever considered the quantity of stitches in a shirt without fear that a general mutiny among females might leave him "without a shirt to his back?" Cannot an ingenious spinner devise a seamless shirt, with its gussets, and wristbands, and collar, and selvages as durable as hemming? The immense work in a shirt is concealed, and yet happily every "better half" prides herself on thinking that she could never do too much towards making good shirts for her "good man." Is it not in his power to relieve her from some of this labor? Can he not form himself and friends into a "society of hearts and manufactures," and get shirts made, as well as washed, by machinery and steam? These inquiries are occasioned by the following letter from a lady to the editor of *The Every-Day Book.*

Sir,

I assure you the *Every-Day Book* is a great favorite among the ladies; and therefore, I send for your insertion a calculation, furnished me by a maiden aunt, of the number of stitches in a plain shirt she made for her grandfather.

Stitching the collar, four rows	3,000
Sewing the ends	500
Buttonholes, and sewing on buttons	150
Sewing on the collar and gathering the neck	1,204
Stitching wristbands	1,228
Sewing the ends	68
Buttonholes	148
Hemming the slits	264
Gathering the sleeves	840
Setting on wristbands	1,468
Stitching shoulder straps, three rows each	1,880
Hemming the neck	390
Sewing the sleeves	2,554
Setting in sleeves and gussets	3,050
Taping the sleeves	1,526
Sewing the seams	848
Setting side gussets	424
Hemming the bottom	1,104
Total number of stitches in my aunt's grandfather's plain shirt	20,646

As witness my hand,
Gertrude Grizenhoofe

Cottenham, near Cambridge
September 1825

The Widow Malone

Did ye hear of the Widow Malone,
>> Ohone!
Who lived in the town of Athlone
>> Alone?
Oh, she melted the hearts
Of the swains in those parts,
So lovely the Widow Malone,
>> Ohone!
So lovely the Widow Malone.

Of lovers she had a full score,
>> Or more;
And fortunes they all had galore,
>> In store;
From the minister down
To the clerk of the crown,
All were courting the Widow Malone,
>> Ohone!
All were courting the Widow Malone.

But so modest was Mrs. Malone,
>> 'Twas known
No one ever could see her alone,
>> Ohone!
Let them ogle and sigh,
They could ne'er catch her eye,
So bashful the Widow Malone,
>> Ohone!
So bashful the Widow Malone.

Till one Mr. O'Brien from Clare,
>> How rare!
It's little for blushing they care
>> Down there;
Put his arm round her waist,
Gave ten kisses in haste,
"Oh," says he, "you're my Molly Malone,
>> My own!"
"Oh," says he, "you're my Molly Malone."

And the widow they all thought so shy,
                My eye!
Ne'er thought of a simper or sigh,
                For why?
But "Lucius," says she,
"Since you've now made so free,
You may marry your Mary Malone,
                Ohone!
You may marry your Mary Malone."

There's a moral contained in my song,
                Not wrong;
And one comfort it's not very long,
                But strong:
If for widows you die,
Learn to kiss, not to sigh,
For they're all like sweet Mistress Malone,
                Ohone!
Oh, they're very like Mistress Malone.

Faith Is a Delicate Endowment

by Francis Hackett

Faith is a precious but delicate endowment. You may say that simple faith is all very well but a man ought to live in the real world and know his way round otherwise he is incapable of handling the existing situation; he is compelled to evade uncomfortable facts. Very true. Quite right. Exactly so. But is it better to be able to face facts at the cost of being a nerveless skeptic or to be something of a simpleton and yet a wholesome man of action, a man of will and character and pep? What is the good of knowing facts if it confuses you and upsets you and undermines everything you've been brought up to believe? What's the use? The skeptic thinks it is very clever to question the things that are of the light in just the same spirit that he questions things that are of the darkness. And, of course, he goes wrong. He is, in the evergreen phrase, destructive and not constructive. You cannot be too careful how you lead people to rationalize. In this world there is rationalization and plenty of it. But is there not also a super-rationalism? And must we not always inculcate super-rationalism when we *know* we possess the true faith?

Fishing

by ELLA WHEELER WILCOX

Maybe this is fun, sitting in the sun,
  With a book and parasol, as my Angler wishes,
While he dips his line in the ocean brine,
  Under the impression that his bait will catch the fishes.

'Tis romantic, yes, but I must confess
  Thoughts of shady rooms at home somehow seem more
    inviting.
But I dare not move—"Quiet, there, my love!"
  Says my Angler, "for I think a monster fish is biting."
Oh, of course it's bliss, but how hot it is!
  And the rock I'm sitting on grows harder every minute;
Still my fisher waits, trying various baits,
  But the basket at his side I see has nothing in it.

Oh, it's just the way to pass a July day,
  Arcadian and sentimental, dreamy, idle, charming,
But how fierce the sunlight falls! and the way that insect
    crawls
  Along my neck and down my back is really quite alarming.
"Any luck?" I gently ask of the Angler at his task.
  "There's something pulling at my line," he says; "I've
    almost caught it."
But when with blistered face we our homeward steps retrace,
  We take the little basket just as empty as we brought it.

· 194 ·

Love Much

by ELLA WHEELER WILCOX

Love much. Earth has enough of bitter in it.
   Cast sweets into its cup whene'er you can.
No heart so hard, but love at last may win it.
   Love is the grand primeval cause of man.
   All hate is foreign to the first great plan.

Love much. Your heart will be led out to slaughter,
   On altars built of envy and deceit.
Love on, love on! 'tis bread upon the water;
   It shall be cast in loaves yet at your feet,
   Unleavened manna, most divinely sweet.

Love much. Your faith will be dethroned and shaken,
   Your trust betrayed by many a fair, false lure.
Remount your faith, and let new trusts awaken.
   Though clouds obscure them, yet the stars are pure;
   Love is a vital force and must endure.

Love much. Men's souls contract with cold suspicion.
   Shine on them with warm love, and they expand.
'Tis love, not creeds, that from a low condition
   Leads mankind up to heights supreme and grand.
   Oh that the world could see and understand!

Love much. There is no waste in freely giving;
   More blessed is it, even, than to receive.
He who loves much alone finds life worth living:
   Love on, through doubt and darkness; and believe
   There is no thing which Love may not achieve.

<hr>

They sin who tell us love can die;
  With life all other passions fly,
    All others are but vanity. . . .
      Love is indestructible,
    Its holy flame forever burneth;
From heaven it came, to heaven
      returneth. . . .
    It soweth here with toil and care,
But the harvest-time of love is there.

          —ROBERT SOUTHEY
        From *The Curse of Kehama*

A Couple

by CARL SANDBURG

He was in Cincinnati, she in Burlington.
He was in a gang of Postal Telegraph linemen.
She was a pot rassler in a boarding house.
"The crying is lonely," she wrote him.
"The same here," he answered.
The winter went by and he came back and they married
And he went away again where rainstorms knocked down
   telegraph poles and wires dropped with frozen sleet.
And again she wrote him, "The crying is lonely."
And again he answered, "The same here."
Their five children are in the public schools.
He votes the Republican ticket and is a taxpayer.
They are known among those who know them
As honest American citizens living honest lives.
Many things that bother other people never bother them.
They have their five children and they are a couple,
A pair of birds that call to each other and satisfy.
As sure as he goes away she writes him, "The crying is lonely"
And he flashes back the old answer, "The same here."
It is a long time since he was a gang lineman at Cincinnati
And she was a pot rassler in a Burlington boarding house;
Yet they never get tired of each other; they are a couple.

Garden

by JOHN GREENLEAF WHITTIER

A hymn for the American Horticultural Society, 1882, originally written
to be sung at an agricultural and horticultural fair in Amesbury in 1853.

O Painter of the fruits and flowers,
   We own Thy wise design,
Whereby these human hands of ours
   May share the work of Thine!

Apart from Thee we plant in vain
  The root and sow the seed;
Thy early and Thy later rain,
  Thy sun and dew we need.

Our toil is sweet with thankfulness,
  Our burden is our boon;
The curse of Earth's gray morning is
  The blessing of its noon.

Why search the wide world everywhere
  For Eden's unknown ground?
That garden of the primal pair
  May nevermore be found.

But, blest by Thee, our patient toil
  May right the ancient wrong,
And give to every clime and soil
  The beauty lost so long.

Our homestead flowers and fruited trees
  May Eden's orchard shame;
We taste the tempting sweets of these
  Like Eve, without her blame.

And, North and South and East and West,
  The pride of every zone,
The fairest, rarest, and the best
  May all be made our own.

Its earliest shrines the young world sought
  In hill-groves and in bowers,
The fittest offerings thither brought
  Were Thy own fruits and flowers.

And still with reverent hands we cull
  Thy gifts each year renewed;
The good is always beautiful,
  The beautiful is good.

"Your Warmest Friend"

A hot letter for Captain Lion, Brighton, the summer of 1825

My dear sir,

I anticipated a sojournment in your "neat little country cottage" during your absence with more pleasure than I expressed when you made me the offer of it. I imagined how much more comfortable I should be there than in my own out-of-town single room. I was mistaken. I have been comfortable nowhere. The malignity of an evil star is against me. I mean the Dog Star.

You recollect the heat I fell into during our Hornsey walk. I have been hot ever since, "hissing hot—think of that Master Brook." I would that thou wert really a brook. I would cleave thy bosom, and, unless thou wert cool to me, I would not acknowledge thee for a true friend.

After returning from the coach wherein you and your lady cousin departed, I "larded the lean earth" to my own house in town. That evening I got into a hackney coach to enjoy your "cool" residence, but it was hot, and there was no "cool of the evening." I went to bed hot, and slept hot all night, and got up hot to a hot tea breakfast, looking all the while on the hot print opposite—Hogarth's "Evening," with the fat hot citizen's wife sweltering between her husband and the New River, the hot little dog looking wistfully into the reachless warm water, her crying hot boy on her husband's stick, the scolding hot sister, and all the other heats of that ever-to-be-warmly-admired engraving. The coldest picture in the room, to my heated eye, was the fruit-piece worked in worsted—worsted in the dog days!

How I got through that hot day I cannot remember. At night, when, according to Addison, "evening shades prevail," the heat prevailed. There were no "cool" shades, and I got no rest, and therefore I got up restless and walked out and saw the morning star, which I suppose was the Dog Star, for I sought coolness and found it not. The sun arose, and it seemed to me there was no atmosphere but burning beams; and the metropolis poured out its heated thousands toward the New River, at Newington; and it was filled with men, and boys, and dogs; and all looked as "comfortable" as live eels in a stew pan.

I am too hot to proceed. What a summer! The very pumps refuse "spring" water, and I suppose we shall have no more till next spring.

My heart melts within me, and I am not so inhuman as to request the servant to broil with this letter to the post office, but I have ordered her to give it to the newsman and ask him to slip it into the first letter-box he passes, and to tell him, if he forgets it, it is of no consequence, and in no hurry; he may take it on to Ludgate Hill, and Mr. Hone, if he please, may print it in his *Every-Day Book*. I dare say he is too hot to write, and this may help to fill up; so that you'll get it, at any rate. I don't care if all the world reads it, for the hot weather is no secret. As Mr. Freeling cannot say that printing a letter is privately conveying it, I shall not get into hot water at the post office.

I am, my dear sir,

Your warmest friend, till winter,

I Fry

Coleman Cottage, Sun Day
P.S. I am told the sight of the postmen in their scarlet coats is not bearable in London; they look *red*-hot.

A Fascinating Description
of the Life of the Eskimo

From *A Voyage to Hudson's Bay by the* Dobbs-Galley *and* California
in the Years 1746 and 1747 for Discovering a Northwest Passage
by HENRY ELLIS, agent for the proprietors in the expedition

On the 8th of July [1747] we sailed with an intention to coast to the northward, but in repassing the shoals, the tide swept us upon a ridge of stones, where our vessel was very near being staved to pieces. While we were in this hazardous situation, there came up to us six canoes of Eskimos with whalebone, which we bought of them. They were very aware of the distress we were in, but so far from taking any advantage of us that they were not only extremely civil, but highly helpful; for when the tide of flood floated us off, an old man, who seemed better acquainted with the place than the rest, paddled before us, pointed out the shoals, and kept in the deep water, so that it was in some measure by his assistance that the *Resolution* not only escaped being lost, but escaped also without suffering any damage. Whatever, therefore, the French writers, or even some of our own, may say, in prejudice, of the character of these poor people, it is but bare justice in us to admit that they treated us not only with humanity, but with great kindness and friendship.

I must confess that I could not help admiring very much not only the industry but the ingenuity of these people, who for want of iron are frequently obliged to make not only the barbs of their arrows, darts and harpoons, but also hatchets and knives, of stones, the teeth of sea horses, or the horns of sea unicorns, which creatures abound here; and it is not easy to say how dextrously they use materials which to us seem so very improper for the purposes to which they employ them. Their needles are also made of the same stuff, notwithstanding which, their clothes are perfectly well sewed, and are not only strong and closely fitting, but very neatly made, in the same manner as those of the people we met with in Hudson's Straits.

"Necessity is the mother of invention"

It is because of this, as well as from the great conformity between them in their language, persons, and customs, that we conclude that they were originally one people; but then it must be acknowledged that these are a more affable, friendly and better disposed sort of folks, as well as more accomplished

An Eskimaux on the N.W. Side of Hudsons Bay

An Eskimaux in his Canoe   *J. Mynde fc.*

artists in those several branches of mechanics which they have been taught by one common mistress—necessity, which is the sole mother of invention amongst them.

It will in some measure justify this observation to remark that the borders of their clothing are commonly fringed with cut leather, and are sometimes hung with fawns' teeth, and the women do not stick out the sides of their boots with whalebone as the other Eskimos do.

They wear a cap made of the skin of a buffalo's tail, which, though it has a horrid appearance, yet is very useful in keeping off the mosquitoes, which in this country are excessively troublesome. It is true that the hair hanging over their faces somewhat obstructs their sight, yet it is easily removed with their hands, and if it were not for this defense, those insects would be insupportable here, as they are in some parts of Lapland. For this purpose their children wear them while they hang at their mothers' backs, when, it must be admitted, they make a most dismal picture, and are apt to raise a shocking idea of the barbarity of these savages, though they are, nevertheless, a very harmless and inoffensive people.

When they go to sea in order to catch fish, they commonly carry with them in their boats a bladder full of train oil, as our people do a dram bottle, and seem to drink the contents with the same relish. Not only that, but also we have sometimes seen them, when their stock was out, draw the very bladder through their teeth with much seeming satisfaction. In all probability, they are convinced by experience of the salutary effects of even this coarse kind of oil in this rigorous climate, which makes them so fond of it. I am rather induced to be of this opinion because I have heard that the inhabitants of St. Kilda, a rocky island on the coast of Scotland, are no less pleased with the oil they make from a fat of Soland geese, which must be very near as rancid.

They also make use of this oil for their lamps, which are made of stone, hollowed out with some difficulty, and as skillfully as can be well expected, considering the tools they work with. For the wick, instead of cotton, which we use, they have recourse to dried goose dung, a very poor substitute indeed, but still better than none.

Making fire by rubbing two sticks together

They have a very dextrous method of kindling fire. They prepare two small pieces of dry wood, which, having made flat, they next make a small hole in each, and having fitted into these holes a little cylindrical piece of wood to which a thong is fastened, they whirl it about with such a velocity that, by rubbing the pieces of wood one against the other, this motion soon sets them on fire. Then by applying the lighted piece of wood to dry moss, in the same manner that we use tinder, they make as great a fire as they please.

What little timber they have is entirely driftwood; and this failing them in the winter, they are obliged to make use of their lamps for their family occasions. A notion has pretty generally prevailed that these people live underground in the winter; but that this is absolutely a mistake appears from the fact that the country in which they live is for the most part one continued rock, and though possibly there may be a considerable depth of soil in some of their valleys, this being frozen almost as hard as that rock, such a manner of living must be to them impracticable.

A Couple of Poems by Twain and Moore

From *Mark Twain's Sketches, New and Old*

Those Evening Bells

by Thomas Moore

Those evening bells! those evening bells!
How many a tale their music tells
Of youth, and home, and that sweet time
When last I heard their soothing chime.

Those joyous hours are passed away;
And many a heart that then was gay,
Within the tomb now darkly dwells,
And hears no more those evening bells.

And so 'twill be when I am gone—
That tuneful peal will still ring on;
While other bards shall walk these dells,
And sing your praise, sweet evening bells.

Those Annual Bills

by Mark Twain

These annual bills! these annual bills!
How many a song their discord trills
Of "truck" consumed, enjoyed, forgot,
Since I was skinned by last year's lot!

Those joyous beans are passed away;
Those onions blithe, O where are they!
Once loved, lost, mourned—*now* vexing ills,
Your shades troop back in annual bills!

And so 'twill be when I'm aground—
These yearly duns will still go round,
While other bards, with frantic quills,
Shall damn and *damn* these annual bills!

The Musical Mice

as told by ROBERT STRAND to B. A. BOTKIN
From *A Treasury of American Anecdotes*
Copyright © 1957 by B. A. Botkin
Reprinted by permission of Curtis Brown, Ltd.

A fellow went into a bar and after he had a couple of drinks he said to the bartender, "Do you want to see something?"

The bartender said, "Sure."

So he took out a tiny piano and a stool and he laid them on the bar.

The bartender said, "That's cute."

Then the fellow said, "Wait, wait, you haven't seen anything yet." And he reached into his vest pocket and he took out a tiny mouse and he sat the mouse down on the stool and said, "Play." And the mouse started to beat out Rachmaninoff and Bach and Brahms and Beethoven.

The bartender said, "That's marvelous! I've never seen anything like it before."

And everyone in the bar started to come up and watch this.

The fellow said, "Aw, you haven't seen anything yet."

And he pulled out another little mouse and he put it next to the piano and said, "Sing." And while the pianist mouse was beating out the rhythm, the singing mouse sang arias from *La Traviata* and from *Tristan and Isolde*, and everybody in the bar was just thunderstruck.

One fellow said, "Do you know, that's the most wonderful thing I've ever seen in my life? I'll give you twenty thousand dollars for that, spot cash."

The bartender said, "Don't sell it. That thing's worth a million dollars on television."

The fellow said, "Aw, I'm going to sell it. I need the money."

So he took the twenty thousand dollars and the other fellow took the two mice and the piano and walked out.

The bartender said, "Boy! Are you crazy! You could have made a fortune with that."

"Aw, don't be silly! It's a phony!"

"What do you mean 'a phony'?"

"That mouse can't sing! The one at the piano is a ventriloquist!"

Crossing the Equator

by JOHN MURRAY from *Six Months in the West Indies in 1825*

About six in the evening of the 17th of January, a sail was discovered to windward on the larboard bow. Shortly afterwards the man on the foretop gallant yard saw that she was making towards us on the other tack. There seemed to be something mysterious in the appearance of this sail and the course she was keeping; unless she came from Sierra Leone, no one could imagine what she was. The captain eyed her with his glass; she was under courses and topsails, with her jibs flying, and a broad pendant at the mast head. Yet she made no signal, and was nearing us fast.

The sun went down into the sea as a great palpable sphere of flame, and the stars came out as stars only come out over the bosom of the central Atlantic. I had been hanging over the windward gangway and gazing on the sea till my eyes swam. (But I recommend that no one follow my example; the draft is very great and is sure to develop any rheumatic tendencies you may accidentally possess.) I thought a fair and languid shape rose ever and anon between the foamy crests of the purple waves, looking Eugenia at me, and beckoning and speaking, though I could not hear, and pointing down to ocean, and then long and steadily to heaven, whereat I trembled and sighed, and fears and suspicious fancies, and thoughts of dead things, and musings of preternatural agencies, absorbed my senses, when on a sudden a tremendous conch roar, issuing from under the bows of the ship, startled me from my reverie.

It was eight o'clock, and a hoarse piratical Atlantic voice hailed us and demanded who we were; the captain answered with his hat off, for it seems he had been on the station before and recognized the awful sound, and having told our name and other log-book particulars, concluded, by requesting His Majesty to come on board. Neptune, for it now appeared to be indeed no other than this awful personage, replied that he could not leave his car that night, but he would visit us the next morning. The conchs Tritonian sounded again, the god rushed by in a flaming chariot like unto a tar barrel, which the sailor heaves upon the forecastle when he tars the newly twisted yarn; and from yards and masts, main top, topgallant and royal, down came an avalanche of water, which laid some

dozen of unwary mariners sprawling in an inundation of Neptunian ichor.

At nine the next morning the king came in through one of the bridle ports. He was seated on what men would have supposed to be a gun carriage, and drawn by four marine monsters. Amphitritty was by his side, and their only child, the heir of the sea, was in her arms. The king was crowned with Atlantic water-flowers, and he bore in his hand the trident which sailors have imitated in the common grange. He was preceded by six Tritons, whom I had so often wished to see and hear after reading Wordsworth's sonnet—*The world is too much with us*—and Mercury came with wings, caduceus and a scroll under his arm. A white bear, who seemed to have come from Regent's Inlet on an iceberg, which melted in latitude 50° and left him to shift for himself, acted as body guard, and another troop of Tritons closed the cavalcade.

We all took off our hats; civil things passed between Neptune and the captain; the man complained that the trades were kept too far to the south now, and the god declared that as he traveled by steam himself, he was wholly unaware of the fact, but that he would order them up forthwith; and then he desired all his children, who had not entered his kingdom's capital province before, to listen to his public crier, and willingly do accordingly.

While I was giving the bear cake to eat, Mercury read an oration, some parts of which were hermetically sealed from my comprehension; however, he urged us to admire Amphitritty, a woman, as he assured us, as remarkable for the "hamiableness" [amiableness] of her disposition, as, we saw, she was for the "helegancy" [elegancy] of her person. He finished by repeating to us youngsters those three invaluable maxims which will carry a man safe through the world.

1. Never heave anything to windward except hot water and ashes.

2. Never drink small beer when you can get strong, unless you like small beer better.

3. Never kiss the maid when you may kiss the mistress, unless, as aforesaid, you happen to like kissing the maid better.

The pageant passed off; but two water bailiffs came and tapped me on the shoulder, with a "You're wanted." It made me think of my debts. They wished to blindfold me, but I was determined to be shaved, like Ney, with my eyes wide open.

As I walked slowly to the forecastle I was considerably washed by a dozen buckets of water sent down upon me from the main top and yard; then I mounted the ladder; at the top stood the doctor on one side and the barber on the other; the medical man felt my pulse, said it fluttered a little, and gave me a saline draft from an eau de cologne bottle, and gently pushed me into a deep purse bag half full of water. Thrice I essayed to get out; thrice the pensile sail tripped me up, and Bear, ungrateful Bear, who was rolling about at the bottom, caught me in an amorous hug, and dallied with me with his tarry palms. At last I doubled him up with a smashing hit in the wind, stood upon him and clambered out, knocked down the shaver, and ran through a Niagara of water to my cabin.

After this, Ducking began in all its forms, under every possible modification of splashing and immersion. There was

the Duck courteous, the Duck oblique, the Duck direct, the
Duck upright, the Duck downright, the bucket Duck, the
tub Duck, the shower Duck, and the Duck and Drake.
          "There was water, water everywhere,
              And not a drop to drink."
A fine water-piece.

But Neptune sent the trades. Full on our larboard quarter
did they blow, every sail was set, the flying fish glided by us,
bonitos and albacores played round the bows, dolphins gleamed
in our wake, ever and anon a shark, and once a great emerald-
colored whale kept us company, till, on the morning of the
29th of January, we made the green shores of Barbados, and
cast our anchor in Carlisle Bay.

◆—◆—◆

Don't Take Your Troubles to Bed
by Edmund Vance Cooke

You may labor your fill, friend of mine, if you will;
    You may worry a bit, if you must;
You may treat your affairs as a series of cares,
    You may live on a scrap and a crust;
But when the day's done, put it out of your head;
Don't take your troubles to bed.

You may batter your way through the thick of the fray,
    You may sweat, you may swear, you may grunt;
You may be a jack-fool if you must, but this rule
    Should ever be kept at the front:—
Don't fight with your pillow, but lay down your head
And kick every worriment out of the bed.

That friend or that foe (which he is, I don't know),
    Whose name we have spoken as Death,
Hovers close to your side, while you run or you ride,
    And he envies the warmth of your breath;
But he turns him away, with a shake of his head,
When he finds that you don't take your troubles to bed.

◆—◆—◆

It Took Sharp Wits to Survive

by P. T. Barnum

From *Cheerio's Book of Days* by Charles K. Field
Copyright, 1940, by Garden City Publishing Co., Inc.

*You speak of me as "sharp-witted"—let me tell you, it took
sharp wits to survive in that early environment of mine!*

Where was that?

*In my native village of Bethel, Connecticut. When I was in
my early teens I left school to work in a grocery store; I
quickly learned that in those days all business was conducted
on the principle of sharp practice. Both sides expected it and
nobody cried "Foul!"*

*I remember a story they told of a grocer who was also a
church deacon. He called downstairs, before breakfast, to
his clerk:*

"John, have you watered the rum?" "Yes sir."

"And sanded the sugar?" "Yes sir."

"And dusted the pepper?" "Yes sir."

"And chicoried the coffee?" "Yes sir."

"Then come up to prayers."

Well, sir, you started up the ladder to fame and fortune when you came to New York, bought the American Museum and popularized such now standard figures as the fat lady, the tattooed man, the human skeleton, the original Siamese twins and so on.

Yes, I gathered curiosities from all over the world, and in my advertisements, of course, I always made them just a little bit more curious.

You old showman, with your jolly deceptions! It's a wonder the public forgave you some of them.

The public loves to be humbugged!

Yes, but after being repeatedly humbugged, no matter in how jolly a fashion, didn't people begin to think everything was a fake?

Yes, some of them did, and thereby made a great mistake. For many persons have such a horror of being "taken in" that they believe everything to be a sham and in this way are continually humbugging themselves! Your cynic is the greatest humbug of all.

There is one amiable deceiver in connection with your business, Mr. Barnum—the adult who pretends to go to the circus on account of the children. Do you recall a bit of old verse which comments slyly upon this bit of humbug?

∗

Old men were there, old women too;
   Middle-aged folks, large and small;
Mamas were there, with their little ones,
   Who wouldn't have come at all
If it hadn't been for the babies dear
   Who wanted so much to see
The panthers and tigers and elephants
   And the wonderful chimpanzee!
        From *Circus Days* by ANNIE H. STREETER

∗

We in the show business are pleased to accept that explanation of the attendance! And I was generally there to greet them. You see, I had really become an international notoriety. People came to see me as well as the circus. Indeed, in Philadelphia, one small boy, going through the menagerie, asked, "Say, Paw, which cage is Barnum in?"

A Letter to the Lord

by LEEWIN B. WILLIAMS from *Talk-Tactics*

A Virginia mountaineer [during the Depression] complained grievously to his minister about the hard times that had been visited upon him. "Things have been going from bad to worse," brooded the man. "I'm behind with taxes, and there's a mortgage due. I'll have to have help or lose the place."

The minister sought to bear up the man's spirit, and suggested that he take his troubles to the Lord. The farmer, simple soul, trudging homeward over his rough acres, suddenly got a bright idea. He would write a letter to the Lord, setting forth his case in detail, and plead for help to carry on the farm. He would need, of course, a few hundred dollars to make a payment on the mortgage, but he would be moderate in his petition, putting down the figure at five hundred.

Having carefully written the letter, he addressed it to "The Lord." For a street address he wrote, "On High," and being not far from the capital, he penned "Washington, D.C." as the last line.

In due course of time the letter, which bore no return address, landed at the Dead Letter office. Amused, the clerk in charge referred the letter to a friend, who, his curiosity whetted, opened the envelope and read the letter. And as he read, he was deeply touched by the simple faith and the sad plight of the mountaineer. Half in humor, half inspired by sympathy, he passed the letter on to a wealthy officeholder, with a suggestion. As a result, the letter went through a number of hands, and a total of three hundred dollars was subscribed to the cause of the mountaineer. This sum the clerk mailed, in three one-hundred dollar bills, to the address given, without comment.

A few days later the mountaineer met the minister, who asked as to his affairs.

"Well, you know what you said about taking my troubles to the Lord," said the man.

"Yes, yes," answered the minister eagerly.

"I did just that, Reverend," continued the man. "I thought it would be easier to get in all facts if I wrote my troubles in a letter. So I told the Lord I needed five hundred dollars, and I got my answer only yesterday."

"Of course, the Lord would answer your prayers," said the minister confidently.

"Yes," agreed the mountaineer, "and it was postmarked Washington, all right, but when I looked in the letter, I found that them crooked politicians over there had opened the envelope and taken out two hundred dollars."

Thoughts in a Yacht

(expressed in parentheses)

Oh! 'tis pleasant to sail in a yacht,
(Rather rough weather this morning we've got,)
Breasting the tide with its billows of foam.
(How glad I shall be when I'm safely at home!)

Oh! 'tis pleasant to sail on the sea,
(Wretchedly ill I shall presently be,)
Watching the broad billows bear us from land.
(Think that it's better to sit than to stand.)

Light as the smoke from the pipe I have lit,
(Think that it's better to stand than to sit,)
Flies the *Fair Rosamond* over the wave.
(Zooks! what a lurch at that moment she gave!)

Sons of the sea-kings, we laugh at the storm;
(Beer? no, I thank you, it's rather too warm;)
Let the winds whistle—(I can't keep my legs—
Oh! the next thing for breakfast is coffee and eggs.)

Let the winds whistle, we love their wild tones;
(Cruel, that smile of the strong-stomached Jones!)
Here at our ease (every minute I dread,
Shifting the thingumbobs over our head.)

Isn't it pleasant, this cruise in a yacht?
(Catch me again in it certainly not!)
Tossing about—(ah! the peril is past,
Thank goodness, we're back in the harbor at last!)

A Gardener's Love Letter

February 14, 1851

My Rosemary,

As *Yew* are the *Pink* of perfection and the *Blossom* of May, I wish to tell *Yew* that my *Heartsease* has been torn up by the *Roots,* and the *Peas* of my *Holm* entirely destroyed since I began to *Pine* after *Yew.*

Yew will perceive that I am a gardener. My name is William Bud. At first I was poor, but by *Shooting* in the *Spring,* and driving a *Carnation* fast, I obtained a *Celery,* and by a little *Cabbaging,* etc., I *Rose* to be master (though something like a *Creeper*) of the whole garden. I have now the full command of the *Stocks* and the *Mint*; I can raise *Ane-mone,* from a *Penny Royal* to a *Plum,* and what my expenditure *Leaves* I put in a *Box* for *Yew.*

If I may, as a *Cock's-comb,* speak of myself, I should say that I am in the *Flower* of manhood — that I am neither a *Standard* nor a *Dwarf,* a *Mushroom* nor a *Maypole.* My nose is of the *Turnip-Reddish* kind, and my locks hang in clusters about my *Ears.* I am often in the company of *Rakes,* and rather fond of *Vine* and *Shrub*—which my *Elders* reprove me for; so I had better *Berry* all this, and as I am a *Branch* of a good *Stock,* with a portly *Bearing,* I well know when and where to make my *Bough.*

So *Lett-uce* act for ourselves and fix an early day for engrafting your fate with mine—which might be made a *Pop-lar* measure; but I think it had better be *Privet,* for *Jon-quil,* the lawyer, says that your old *Crab* of a father, who never did a *Li-lac,* when he wanted to part us, means to take the *Elm* in his own hands in this matter; but if he does, and *Bul-lace* me at all, I will not be *Sloe* in settling his *Ash,* and I will be such a *Thorn* in his side that the day he does it shall be one of the worst *Dais-y* ever saw.

But I must sow no seeds of discord; for I am certain that we should make a very nice *Pear,* and never repent even when we became *Sage* by *Thyme.* *Yew* would be the *Balm* of my life, and I should be the *Balsam* of yours; so that people that might call us *Green* now would call us *Evergreen* hereafter.

And now, *Sweet Peas* be with *Yew*; and if he who tries at it tears me from *Yew,* I shall become a *Melon-Cauli-flower* and wither away. My tongue will always be a *Scarlet Runner* in your praise; for I have planted my *Hopes* in *Yew,* and I only live for the *Thyme* when I may hear from your own *Tu-lips* that I am your *Sweet William,* and not your *Weeping Will-ow.*

The Lost Theater Tickets

From *Champagne Before Breakfast* by HY GARDNER
Copyright, 1954, by HY GARDNER
Reprinted by permission of Holt, Rinehart and Winston, Inc.

One of the real classic Broadway yarns is spun by John Shubert, who claims it actually happened to a Shubert employee.

A short, slightly stooped man wearing a well-pressed suit stepped up to the box office of one of the Broadway legitimate theaters about ten minutes before curtain time. "May I speak to the treasurer, please?" he asked the ticket taker.

"Jack, front and center," the busy man growled, "get Sam. A guy here wants to make with some words."

In a few moments a quizzical, shirt-sleeved gent peered from behind the "reservation" window. "Something you wanted, bud?" he asked.

"Yes, sir, if you don't mind. I'd like my four seats for tonight's show—seats D12, 14, 16 and 18. You see, I haven't got the tickets with me, but I did take down the locations."

"Look, mister, if you're careless, don't give me ulcers. Now trot along."

"Please, I'll make you a proposition. Send an usher down to prove that D12, 14, 16 and 18 are unoccupied. If they're empty, let my party use them. And what's more, to show my sincerity I'll give you fifty dollars to keep as security until the show is over."

The usher checked and reported the seats were unoccupied.

"Okay," the treasurer said, "I'll pass you in but I'm taking your fifty and if anyone shows up with the tickets not only will you be thrown out—but to show my sincerity I'll keep the fifty."

The party took their seats and during intermission filed into the lobby for a smoke. Graciously the treasurer beckoned the little man with the well-pressed suit to join him in his office.

"Mister," he smiled, "I've been in this racket a long time and I always thought I could spot a gate-crasher with half a sleepy eye open. You fooled me and I'm sorry if I was rough on you. It looks like you told a really legit story. We won't wait until the next act is over—here's your fifty bucks."

"That's mighty thoughtful of you and I appreciate it," was the reply. "It really wasn't my carelessness though; misplacing the tickets was my son's fault. I'm teaching the boy my business, and while we were working on a job this morning I ran across the tickets and told him to stick them into my vest pocket. Instead he got confused and slipped them into our client's vest pocket—now they're gone forever."

"What do you mean they're gone forever—say, what business are you in anyway?"

"Oh, I'm sorry. I thought I told you," the little man apologized, "I'm an undertaker. Here, take my card, maybe I can do something for you sometime."

ᴐᴠᴐᴠᴐ

Evasion of the Postal Laws
From *Ten Years among the Mail Bags* by J. HOLBROOK

Before the adoption of the present rates of postage, much ingenuity was displayed in making newspapers the vehicles of such information as should legitimately have been conveyed by letters. Various devices were employed to effect this object.

As the law strictly prohibited writing upon papers, requiring that such newspapers should be charged with letter postage, the problem was to convey information by their means without infringing the letter of the law.

Sometimes a sentence or a paragraph was selected, some of the letters of which were crossed out in such a manner that the letters left legible conveyed the meaning which the operator intended. By such transmuting process, pugnacious editorials were converted into epistles of the mildest and most affectionate description, and public news of an important character not unfrequently contracted into a channel for the conveyance of domestic intelligence.

As the constructions of the law on this subject, by the officers of the Department, became more and more stringent, the most amusing and ingenious inventions to get beyond their reach were resorted to.

For instance, marking an advertisement or other notice, with a pen or pencil, having been declared a violation of law, attention was sometimes called to such notices by cutting round them on three sides, thus making a sort of flap, and doubling it back on the side left uncut. In one case, which now occurs to the author, a notice served in that way, thus producing a hole in the paper, had the strikingly appropriate caption of "A good Opening!"

The vacancy produced in the paper, in such a case, of course attracted the attention of the person who received it, and *that* advertisement was sure to be read, if no other.

Hieroglyphics were sometimes employed for conveying contraband ideas. The following will answer as a specimen of this class of attempted evasions. It was neatly drawn on the margin of a newspaper which came to a Western post office from a town in New England.

The meaning will of course be readily understood by the reader—
"Children all well!"

Such specimens of the fine arts are seldom attempted under the
present low rates of postage, as the saving of two cents would hardly
pay for the required time or labor. But there are those even nowadays,
who, for that paltry consideration, are found willing to compromise
their consciences, if indeed they have any, by resorting to some of the
less laborious methods, in attempting to carry out their prudential
designs.

The Conservative

by Edmund Vance Cooke

At twenty, as you proudly stood
And read your thesis, "Brotherhood,"
If I remember right, you saw
The fatuous faults of social law.

At twenty-five you braved the storm
And dug the trenches of Reform,
Stung by some gadfly in your breast
Which would not let your spirit rest.

At thirty-five you made a pause
To sum the columns of The Cause;
You noted, with unwilling eye,
The heedless world had passed you by.

At forty you had always known
Man owes a duty to His Own.
Man's life is as man's life is made;
The game is fair, if fairly played.

At fifty, after years of stress
You bore the banner of Success.
All men have virtues, all have sins,
And God is with the man who wins.

At sixty, from your captured heights
You fly the flag of Vested Rights,
Bounded by bonds collectable,
And hopelessly respectable!

It Was Midnight on the Ocean

by Harry K. McClintock and Sterling Sherwin
Copyright 1932 by Southern Music Publishing Co., Inc.
Copyright renewed. Used by permission.

Now I know a little ditty, it's as crazy as can be;
The guy who wrote it said so as he handed it to me.
I found I couldn't use it, just because it sounded blue;
And that's the very reason why I'm handing it to you.

It's the song the alligators sing while coming through the rye;

As they serenade the elephants up in the trees so high;
The ice man hums this ditty, as he shovels in the coal;
And the monkeys join the chorus up around the Northern
    Pole.

It was midnight on the ocean, not a streetcar was in sight;
The sun was shining brightly for it rained all day that night.
'Twas a summer night in winter and the rain was snowing fast,
And a barefoot boy with shoes on stood a-sitting on the grass.

While the organ pealed potatoes, lard was rendered by the
    choir;
The sexton wrung the dishrag, someone set the church on fire;
"Holy Smoke!" the preacher shouted, in the rain he lost his
    hair;
Now his head resembles heaven, for there is no parting there.

It was midnight on the ocean, not a horsecar was in sight,
As I stepped into the drugstore, to get myself a light;
The man behind the counter was a woman, old and gray,
Who used to peddle shoestrings on the road to Mandalay.

"Oh, good evening, sire," the woman said, and her eyes were
    bright with tears,
As she put her head beneath her feet and stood that way for
    years.
Her children six were orphans, except one big tiny tot,
Who lived in the house across the street above a vacant lot.

The Firm of Grin and Barrett

by SAM WALTER FOSS from *Songs of the Average Man*
Lothrop, Lee & Shepard Company

No financial throe volcanic
　Ever yet was known to scare it;
Never yet has any panic
　Scared the firm of Grin and Barrett.
From the flurry and the fluster,
　From the ruin and the crashes,
They arise in brighter lustre,
　Like the phoenix from his ashes.
When the banks and corporations
　Quake with fear, they do not share it;
Smiling through all perturbations
　Goes the firm of Grin and Barrett.
　　　　Grin and Barrett,
　　　　Who can scare it?
Scare the firm of Grin and Barrett?

When the tide-sweep of reverses
　Smites them, firm they stand and dare it
Without wailings, tears, or curses,
　This stout firm of Grin and Barrett.
Even should their house go under
　In the flood and inundation,
Calm they stand amid the thunder
　Without noise or demonstration.
And, when sackcloth is the fashion,
　With a patient smile they wear it,
Without petulance or passion,
　This old firm of Grin and Barrett.
　　　　Grin and Barrett,
　　　　Who can scare it?
Scare the firm of Grin and Barrett?

When the other firms show dizziness,
　Here's a house that does not share it.
Wouldn't you like to join the business?
　Join the firm of Grin and Barrett?
Give your strength that does not murmur,
　And your nerve that does not falter,
And you've joined a house that's firmer
　Than the old rock of Gibraltar.

They have won a good prosperity;
    Why not join the firm and share it?
Step, young fellow, with celerity;
    Join the firm of Grin and Barrett.
        Grin and Barrett,
        Who can scare it?
Scare the firm of Grin and Barrett?

The Declaration
by JOHN GODFREY SAXE

"Faith! Women are riddles!" I muttered one day,
    As I sat by my beautiful Bess;
It seems very queer that whatever they say,
    Their meaning no mortal can guess.

I knew that she loved me by many a sign
    That served her affection to show;
But when I suggested, will Betty be mine?
    Confound her! She answered me "No!"

'Tis the way with the sex—so I often had heard—
    And thus their assent they express;
But I couldn't but think it extremely absurd
    That a "No" was the same as a "Yes".

So I asked her again, with my heart in a whirl,
    And said, "Do not answer me so!"
When twice in succession the mischievous girl
    Repeated that odious "No".

"There," she said, with a laugh, "that is certainly plain;
    And your hearing is not overnice,
Or you wouldn't have forced me to say it again;
    For I think I have spoken it twice."

"I see," I exclaimed, as I clasped in my own
    The hand of my beautiful Bess;
"I now recollect—what the grammar has shown—
    Two negatives equal a "Yes".

A Poem for the Editor

from Mark Twain's Sketches

To Mr. Mark Twain: The within parson, which I have set to poetry under the name and style of "He Done His Level Best," was one among the whitest men I ever see, and it an't every man that knowed him that can find it in his heart to say he's glad the poor cuss is busted and gone home to the States. He was here in an early day, and he was the handyest man about takin' holt of anything that come along you most ever see, I judge. He was a cheerful, stirrin' cretur, always doin' somethin', and no man can say he ever see him do anything by halvers. Preachin' was his nateral gait, but he warn't a man to lay back and twidle his thumbs because there didn't happen to be nothin' doin' in his own especial line—no, sir, he was a man who would meander forth and stir up something for hisself. His last acts was to go his pile on "kings-*and*" (calklatin' to fill, but which he didn't fill), when there was a "flush" out agin him, and naterally, you see, he went under. And so he was cleaned out, as you may say, and he struck the home-trail, cheerful but flat broke. I knowed this talonted man in Arkansaw, and if you would print this humbly tribute to his gorgis abilities, you would greatly obleege his onhappy friend.

HE DONE HIS LEVEL BEST.

Was he a mining on the flat—
    He done it with a zest;
Was he a leading of the choir—
    He done his level best.

If he'd a reg'lar task to do,
    He never took no rest;
Or if 'twas off-and-on—the same—
    He done his level best.

If he was preachin' on his beat,
    He'd tramp from east to west,
And north to south—in cold and heat
    He done his level best.

He'd yank a sinner outen (Hades),*
And land him with the blest;
Then snatch a prayer'n waltz in again,
And do his level best.

He'd cuss and sing and howl and pray,
And dance and drink and jest,
And lie and steal—all one to him—
He done his level best.

Whate'er this man was sot to do,
He done it with a zest;
No matter *what* his contract was,
HE'D DO HIS LEVEL BEST.

Verily, this man *was* gifted with "gorgis abilities," and it is a
happiness to me to embalm the memory of their lustre in these
columns. If it were not that the poet crop is unusually large and
rank in California this year, I would encourage you to continue
writing, Simon Wheeler; but, as it is, perhaps it might be too risky
in you to enter against so much opposition.

A Cunning Astrologer

From *The Percy Anecdotes*

An astrologer in the reign of Louis the XIth of France, having
foretold something disagreeable to the king, his majesty, in
revenge, resolved to have him killed. The next day he sent for
the astrologer, and ordered the people about him, at a signal
given, to throw the astrologer out of the window.

As soon as the king saw him, "You that pretend," said he,
"to be such a wise man, and know so perfectly the fate of
others, inform me a little what will be your own, and how
long you have to live."

The astrologer, who now began to apprehend some danger,
answered with great presence of mind, "I know my destiny,
and am certain I shall die three days before your majesty."

---

*Here I have taken a slight liberty with the original MS. "Hades" does not make
such good metre as the other word of one syllable, but it sounds better.

The king, on hearing this, was so far from having him thrown out of the window that, on the contrary, he took particular care not to suffer him to want anything, and did all that was possible to retard the death of one whom he was likely so soon to follow.

The Old Golfer Dies

by EDGAR A. GUEST, from *The Friendly Way*
Copyright 1931 by The Reilly & Lee Company

Old Sandy was a dying man; the doctor shook his head.
"You'd better call the family in," unto the nurse he said.
"He tries to speak," the nurse replied, and bending low she heard:
"I want the boys, I want the boys—for them I have a word."

His loved ones gathered round his bed and watched him weaker grow.
"I must," he gasped, "say something to the boys before I go."
"They're coming, Pa; they'll soon be here," a daughter softly said,
"Give me the message you would leave," but Sandy shook his head.

They wondered what he had to tell and what was on his mind,
But none could guess the counsel which he wished to leave behind.
"The boys, the boys," he spoke again, " 'tis them I wish to see.
I hope they will get here in time to hearken unto me."

Into the room they came at last, the old man called them near;
"My boys," said he in faltering tones, "not long will I be here,
But this I want to say to you once more before I die:
Never play your brassie when you have a down-hill lie!"

* * *

This volume in my hand, I hold a charm
Which lifts me out of reach of wrong or harm.
I sail away from trouble; and most blessed
Of every blessing, can myself forget:
Can rise above the instance low and poor
Into the mighty law that governs yet.

From the *London Spectator*
January 16, 1886 — by F.M.P.